I0762813

# BEHIND THE BOTTLE

# JACK DANIEL'S

Published by Cider Mill Press, an imprint of HarperCollins Focus LLC, 501 Nelson Place, Nashville, TN 37214 USA.



13-Digit ISBN: 978-1-40034-757-5
10-Digit ISBN: 1-40034-757-2

Books published by Cider Mill Press Book Publishers are available at special discounts for bulk purchases in the United States by corporations, institutions, and other organizations. For more information, please contact the publisher.

cidermillpress.com



HarperCollins Publishers, Macken House, 39/40 Mayor Street Upper,
Dublin 1, D01 C9W8, Ireland (https://www.harpercollins.com)

Typography: Zenon, Nicholas, Neue Haas Unica W1G

Image Credits: Pages 4–5, 18, 34, 59, 60–61, 110–111, 120, 121, 124–125, 134–135, 136, 144–145, 155, 163, 181, 189, 199, 202, 203, 206, 218–219, 220–221, 222–223, 224–225, and 242–243 courtesy of Richard Thomas; Pages 8, 51, 95, 192, 193, 230–231, 233, 234–235, 281, 282–283 used under official license from Shutterstock. Pages 12–13, 14, 26, 30–31, 38–39, 40, 46, 56, 62, 71, 81, 84, 86, 97, 98, 101, 107, 108–109, 112–113, 119, 130–131, 132, 137 (bottom), 164, 174–175, 176, 179, 180, 184–185, 188, 194, 199, 200–201, 212, 228, 237, 238–239, 241, 246, 247, 250, 251, 253, 254, 257, 259, 260, 261, 262–263, 266, 267, 277, and 279 courtesy of Brown-Forman; Pages 20–21 courtesy of Nearest Green Distillery; Page 29 courtesy of Tennessee State Library & Archives, "Temperance Rally!", Library Broadside Collection, 1814-2010, Box 5, Folder 7, ID# 36539; Page 42 courtesy of Tennessee State Library & Archives, "Trademark registration by Lem Motlow for the phrase "Old No. 7"," 1908 October 12, RG 225, Trademark Registrations, 36529_01; Pages 45 and 52 courtesy of the St. Louis Post Dispatch; Pages 50, 226, 244–245, 268–269, 272–273, and 274–275 used under official license from Adobe Stock; Pages 74 and 75 courtesy of National Parks Service-Olmstead Photograph Album Collection; Pages 90 (Michael Ochs Archives), 92 (Henry Diltz), 104 (Eamonn McCabe/Popperfoto), and 105 (Paul Natkin) used under official license from Getty Images; Page 103 (top) courtesy of John Moran and Amber Van Bossel; Page 103 (bottom) courtesy of Marta Byrdziak and Amber Van Bossel; Page 137 (top) courtesy of Tennessee State Library & Archives, Jack Daniel's Hollow, Library Photograph Collection, Oversize, Drawer 10, ID# 31816; Pages 138–139 courtesy of Tennessee State Library & Archives, Jack Daniel's Distillery, Library Photograph Collection, Oversize, Drawer 10, ID# 31815; Page 214 courtesy of Independent Stave Compnay; All other images courtesy of John Whalen Jr./Cider Mill Press.

Printed in Malaysia
25 26 27 28 29 PJM 5 4 3 2 1
First Edition

# BEHIND THE BOTTLE

# JACK DANIEL'S

RICHARD THOMAS

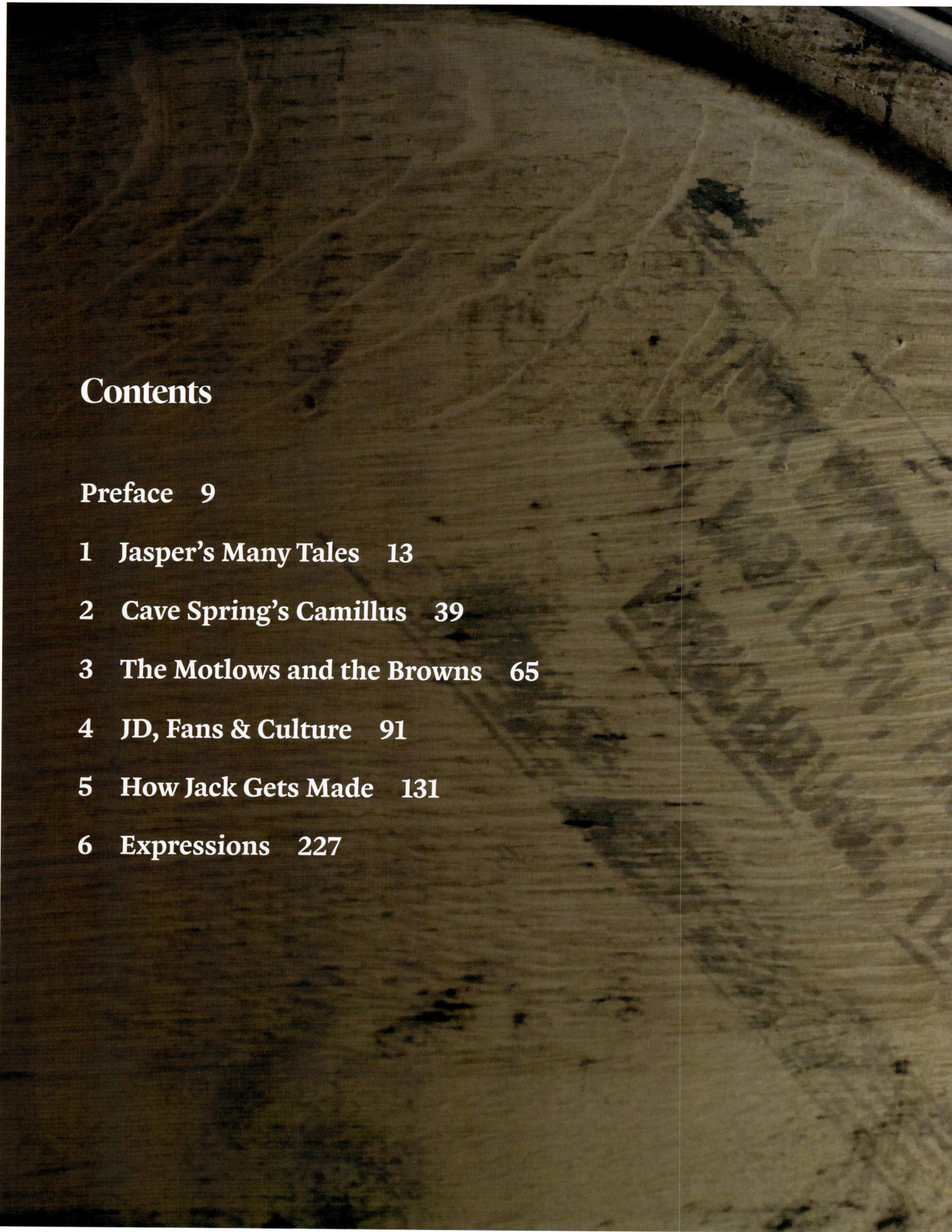

# Contents

JACK DANIEL'S
Coca-Cola
BBQ

WELCOME TO
LYNCHBURG
TENNESSEE

# Preface

When I was approached with the idea of doing a book about Jack Daniel's, my initial reaction was to think of myself as an odd choice. After all, I'm a Kentucky horse farmer's son. Although I look on our sister state of Tennessee with some affection, I grew up in an environment that thought of the regional whiskeys this way: bourbon is our thing and Jack Daniel's is their thing. And that is the nice way of putting it. That colored my perception of all things Tennessee Whiskey for decades, and I came around to a rediscovery of Jack Daniel's only in my 30s.

Yet at the time of the pitch, I had just finished my previous work, *Whiskey Stories*. For that book, I traveled for the third time to the big distillery in that little town of Lynchburg, Tennessee, to do research on some of the tall tales surrounding Jack Daniel, as well as some of the true crime attached to his nephew and successor, Lem Motlow. The idea of following up and building on that work was exciting, so I pounced. And, of course, that led me back to Lynchburg.

Two biographies of Jack Daniel have been written, which is two more than most whiskey distillers get, even when those distillers are the stuff of legend. The first, Ben A. Green's *Jack Daniel's Legacy*, was written in the folksy style that was so prevalent in popular Southern historiography in the mid-twentieth century. I've been told it is (or at least was) required reading for executives at Brown-Forman Corporation, which owns Jack Daniel's, but I think it is in some ways outdated. Peter Krass challenged some of Green's narrative in his 2004 *Blood and Whiskey: The Life and Times of Jack Daniel*. It is a more modern account, and some of Krass's challenges have become not just broadly accepted but part of the official story.

Although no biography has been published about Lem Motlow, putting together the broad strokes of his life was straightforward enough. He was a prominent supporting character in the last stages of Jack Daniel's life, and as a main character he was mired in criminal proceedings during the 1920s, and then a prime mover in the repeal of Prohibition and the reestablishment of the Jack Daniel's Distillery thereafter. From there, the company narrative moves on to Motlow's sons, Brown-Forman, and then into my own lifetime.

But this book is not primarily a company history, nor was it intended to be. Instead, it is more of a drinker's and fan's experience guide. The history matters, and I have tried to offer my own insights into it, but the chapters dealing with the company's backstory are the shortest. The larger share of the book, and the most in-depth behind-the-scenes-look at the distillery that has ever appeared in print, consists of how Jack Daniel's is made, what to expect from the company on bar and liquor store shelves, and the cultural aspects of a brand that rivals any in the world for its resonance. Along the way, I have been able to correct some mistakes that I encountered and have been reprinted time and time again, such as Jack Daniel's allegedly being shuttered during the Second World War.

Two items of news broke pertaining to Jack Daniel's while I was writing. First, the company was pushed off its longtime perch as America's best-selling whiskey and the world's second-best seller by Jim Beam. Kentucky bourbon's top whiskey maker first seized the spot in 2022 and then, according to early 2024 reports, Beam consolidated that position in 2023, and it looks likely that Beam will continue to improve on its lead through 2024. This is the kind of news that only those who follow whiskey as a business care about, but those of us who do know it could signal changes with how Jack Daniel's tends to its business and competes in the marketplace in the future. Even if Beam now sells more whiskey, Jack Daniel's remains a cultural force in a way that is almost more important than drinks sales.

The other news was that Jack Daniel's parent company, Brown-Forman, abandoned its diversity, equity, and inclusion (DEI) policy in August 2024. The announcement was met with widespread criticism in the media, especially among drinks writers. I am not privy to the corporation's internal deliberations, but as an observer of politics in Tennessee and especially Kentucky, I am dismayed at the possibility that the company might have bowed to bullying from croakers in those statehouses, never mind from certain social media trolls. That said, I also have not forgotten that four of the most prominent women in American whiskey today—Elizabeth McCall, Marianne Eaves, Jackie Zykan, and Lexie Phillips—either work for Brown-Forman now or first entered the spotlight as a whiskey maker while working for them. The last of that quartet, Phillips, is currently making whiskey down in Lynchburg.

Fawn Weaver's book *Love & Whiskey* is about her experiences researching the story of Nathan Green, the man who, first as a slave and then a freedman, taught Jack Daniel how to make whiskey, was published very late in my work on the first draft of this book. Although I address Green and try to place him in the wider context of skilled enslaved distillery workers in the South (that story is only beginning to be told), I decided I did not have the time necessary to read and properly digest Weaver's work, so I set it aside. I look forward to reading *Love & Whiskey*, and the public relations firm working for her whiskey company, Uncle Nearest, sent me some photos of the Call farmhouse, but it was not a resource for this work.

Symbolic of the cultural reach of Jack Daniel's and its black labeled Old No. 7 whiskey is just how many nicknames there are for it: JD, Mr. Jack's Whiskey, or simply Jack. In the interest of sidestepping tedium, I freely used all these expressions and treated them as interchangeable.

The final bit of field work for the book I left until this late stage, as I type the literal final words of it. In my research I discovered that Mary Avon Motlow Boyd, Lem Motlow's daughter and the sister of Reagor and Dan Evans, was laid to rest in my hometown of Lexington, Kentucky, some quarter-century ago. That cemetery is just two miles from my doorstep. So, I am off to walk over there and find her headstone.

—September 22, 2024

# Jasper's Many Tales

Despite American whiskey lubricating so many tall tales about its own industry, its brands are replete with the names of real people: Jim Beam, George Dickel, and Evan Williams, just to name a few. Moreover, the stories often told about these whiskey men are usually more authentic than fictional. While the legend that Elijah Craig invented bourbon stubbornly refuses to die, much of what is said about Evan Williams (nowadays at least) is accurate, and there was never much malarky surrounding the biography of James Beauregard Beam.

In the twenty-first century, only one name in whiskey has just as much folklore as fact attached to it, standing as the enduring example of the maxim "when the legend becomes fact, print the legend"—Jack Daniel. Keep in mind that Jack Daniel's Tennessee Whiskey was the biggest whiskey brand in America for decades and that it is still the third largest worldwide, and it is no surprise that some tall tales remain attached to what was Daniel's rather short personage. And even less surprising when one considers the man's vanity. Modern biographers and experts cannot conclusively prove many details of the man's story. Basic issues such as when he was born or why he died linger as little more than educated opinion.

Take the matter of his birth. Some references place the date in 1846, but Daniel's first biographer, Ben A. Green, claimed 1849, while others say 1850. A fixture of the Jack Daniel story is that his mother, Lucinda, died due to complications from delivering baby Jasper (Jack's legal first name), and the tombstone of his parents indicates that Lucinda died on January 29, 1847. That would point to 1846 as the birth year.

One yarn about the confusion surrounding the birthdate is that Daniel himself started fudging it when he reached middle age. Some may counter by asking, "Why would a man shave just two or three years off his age?" Clearly, those people have never spent much time on a dating app.

If details such as this one remain debatable, the broad strokes of Daniel's birth and childhood are not. He was born the youngest of 10 children near antebellum Lynchburg, Tennessee, the town that would be his lifelong home. As previously described, his mother died early in his life, but his father, Calaway, was there for him. Calaway is a part of Daniel's story that I think is neglected. Daniel's boyhood was spent in what were good material circumstances for the place and times. According to Daniel's biographer Peter Krass, Calaway Daniel owned several slaves and a couple hundred acres of land. That made him a substantial farmer, especially in what was then Lincoln County, on the periphery of Middle Tennessee and nestled up against the Highland Rim.

Calaway remarried, the widower marrying 31-year-old Matilda VanZandt in 1851. They had three more children together, one of which died, giving Jack two younger half-sisters. The wicked stepmother is an old trope, but all the family stories agree that there was no love lost between Matilda and her stepson Jack. The question is not whether the relationship was good or not, but just how bad it was. The story often told is that Daniel ran away from home and embarked on his whiskey career to get away from her, and while animosity could very well have been a factor, I believe there is more to it than just that.

Whether he was born in 1846 or 1849, Jack Daniel was in his teens during the Civil War. With so many schoolbooks and films focused on the war in Virginia, the popular imagination forgets that Tennessee saw almost as much strife as the Old Dominion. The Battle of Stones River may not have had the sheer number of dead and wounded as Gettysburg, but the scene was equally savage—one in three of the men who fought there became a casualty. That battle took place just 45 miles north of Lynchburg. The Army of the Cumberland (USA), under Major General William S. Rosecrans, would tromp right through the area during the Tullahoma Campaign of 1863, skillfully maneuvering Braxton Bragg's rebel Army of Tennessee out of its defensive positions while hardly firing a shot. The violence would catch up with Johnny Reb and Billy Yank later, at the Battle of Chickamauga.

But what mattered much more than the clash of great armies to the Daniel family farm and its neighbors was the reality of living in what was, as the war progressed, the rear of the Confederate Army, then the No Man's Land between the two armies, and finally the rear area of the Union forces. Through 1862, commissary agents from both the Confederate government (working to supply the army of Robert E. Lee) and from the local army under Bragg would have been a familiar sight to area farmers, the requisitions paid in Confederate paper money that became more worthless with each passing season. A farmer enjoyed little or no say in what the army took: if the commissaries didn't leave you with enough corn to feed your livestock through the winter, too bad. And that assumes they left you any livestock to feed. Bragg's defeat at Stones River in January 1863 and his subsequent retreat to Tullahoma and the Highland Rim added Union patrols and raids to the woes of regional farmers.

As bad as having produce forcibly taken away was how the agricultural workforce dried up. Young Tennessee men, including some of Daniel's older brothers, either enlisted or, in the case of the Confederacy, were conscripted into the ranks. Emancipation meant the enslaved workforce mostly evaporated. The armies also requisitioned horses and mules. In an era when farms ran on muscle power, Middle Tennessee was denuded of it.

Throughout history, armies have been worse than locusts, and a farmer's only real hope has been that the armies move on. Middle Tennessee was a major battleground for two whole years and remained the site of frequent raids and counterraids until the end of the war. Perhaps worse were the guerillas or outright bandits that mushroomed across Tennessee, as the war left many areas in a state of lawlessness.

Most farmers in Tennessee were ruined by the war. Calaway Daniel was no exception, which was how he met his end in January 1863, in the aftermath of Stones River. Much has been made of what happened next, when Jack Daniel ran away from his stepmother's home and took up work with a neighbor, Dan Call. These were formative years for the teenaged Daniel, set in the larger context of war, destitution, and the loss of his father.

Depending on the year one assigns for his birth, Daniel was either in his early or middle teens at the time of his father's passing, and boys went to work much earlier in those days. To cite just one famous example, Andrew Carnegie went to work at age 13, changing spools of thread in a Pittsburgh cotton mill. In his autobiography, Carnegie wrote that he worked in that cotton mill 12 hours a day, six days a week. The 1870 census found that one in eight American children were employed in real jobs and earning wages.

So, despite being the youngest of the brood from Calaway's first marriage, Daniel was old enough to work. Matilda stayed on the Daniel farm with Daniel's two half-sisters to care for and, in keeping with the times, was soon looking to remarry. Brand historian Nelson Eddy indicated that Daniel financially supported his half-sisters in the years after he left, which hardly suggests strong ill will. As much as he may have wanted to get away from his stepmother, it is not hard to see that grief and economic necessity drove him to work with Call as much as anything else.

Tales of Daniel running away from home at the age of seven are exaggerated. Krass maintains that Daniel was known to be living with his father and even attending school in 1860. The official company timeline shows 1864 as the year Daniel left home.

Besides his work as a distiller, Dan Call was a farmer, the owner of a general store, and a lay Lutheran preacher. He served in the Confederate cavalry force and did not come home until after the war, so it is possible that his wife, Mary, may have been the one who made the decision to take Daniel in. And that's

3G 49
DAN CALL FARM
Dan Call, Lutheran lay minister and a Confederate soldier housed a young Jasper "Jack" Daniel at this farm. Daniel learned the tasks and tricks of the trade from Call's enslaved distiller Nearest Green (born c. 1820), who Call described as "the best whiskey maker that I know." When Daniel became a full partner in the distillery in 1866, and later established his own distillery in 1875, he hired three of Green's sons, ensuring that the legacy of African American whiskey - making would shape his product. Many generations of Green's descendants continued to work for the distillery. Nearest Green is considered the first known African American master distiller of Tennessee Whiskey.
TENNESSEE HISTORICAL COMMISSION

just as well, since running the distilling business during the war years would have made Dan a criminal in the eyes of the Confederate government.

Unlike the federal government, which embraced the whiskey industry and taxed it to support the war effort, the Confederate government banned distilling. They did this because both the grain for fermenting and the copper used to make stills were in short supply in the South throughout the war. Looking with a studied eye at the old distilling site on the Dan Call property, one notices that it is hidden away in a wooded hollow—a place where no one would unsuspectingly stumble upon it.

Call's antebellum distilling business was one step removed from the farmer-distiller model that would have characterized the whiskey of the previous generation. Call used his own surplus grain, as well as what surplus he could buy up from surrounding farmers, to make his whiskey. Whiskey is, in a sense, condensed grain, but as alcohol is easier to move and safe from both pests and spoilage.

Initially employed as a farmhand and around the store, Daniel soon gravitated toward the distilling arm of Call's enterprises, and it isn't hard to see why. As a full-grown man, Daniel stood a mere 5'2", five inches shorter than the average male in his day. I imagine he understood that he was not physically built for the kind of yeoman's life his father had led, and we know he was ambitious. Given his choices, the benefits of producing whiskey were obvious to him.

This is where he would have become intimate with Nathan "Nearest" Green, the actual hands-on distiller in Call's business. In 1866, Green was a freedman in his middle 20s with a wife, Harriet, and two boys (the first two of his nine children). It was from Green, not Call, that Daniel learned the techniques behind making whiskey.

Nathan Green's story was never really a secret, or at least not a secret anyone was trying to keep. Daniel is known to have named Green as the man who taught him about making whiskey, and he would later employ not just Nathan Green, but also three of Green's sons. Green's skills and role in the rise of Jack Daniel's whiskey were well understood by Daniel's contemporaries, and that knowledge hasn't faded away. Green's descendants have counted among the many generational employees of Jack Daniel's, a tradition that continues to this very day. Green's role as one of Daniel's mentors was highlighted in Ben Green's (no relation) *Jack Daniel's Legacy*, published in 1967 (a 50th anniversary printing came out in 2017). The relationship was also extensively detailed in Peter Krass's 2004 biography of Daniel, *Blood & Whiskey*. Far from being

# Jack Daniel, Nathan Green, and the Stories Yet to Be Told

The biggest Jack Daniel's media story of modern times wasn't about a distillery expansion project, a new expression, or even an overturned truck on the highway destroying hundreds of thousands of dollars' worth of whiskey. Starting in 2016 and continuing for years after, the dominant, continuing headline regarding Jack Daniel's was that Daniel had been taught how to make whiskey by a slave. Those headlines and even one or two of the stories attached to them were sometimes sensationalized, implying that the prominent place a slave held in the foundation story of America's most popular whiskey had been forgotten at best and suppressed at worst. A better word to describe it is "overlooked," but overlooked mostly by that selfsame media industry, less so by the people most directly concerned.

The African American at the center of it all was Nathan Green, a slave owned by a labor company. Green was hired out to Dan Call, Daniel's employer, mentor, and later business partner. Starting as an odd jobs hand, Daniel gravitated to the distillery and eventually came to focus on it. Up to 2016, stories of this time said that Daniel learned to make whiskey while working for Call, which is true in a broad sense. To say he learned *from* Call would have been false. Green was already a skilled distiller, despite being only slightly older than Daniel, and it was Green rather than Call who taught Daniel how to actually make whiskey. Key parts of that education were the importance of a good water source and the step of charcoal mellowing, both of which continue to figure prominently in the Jack Daniel's production process today. Green was freed during the Civil War and continued to work, for first Call and then Daniel, after Daniel and Call formed their partnership. When Daniel went into business for himself, Nathan Green did not follow him, but some of his children did.

Green's role in training the young Jack Daniel as a whiskey man was never a secret. Ben Green's official biography, *Jack Daniel's Legacy* mentions Nathan Green (not related to the author) and his descendants many times. He also figured prominently in Peter Krass's biography of Daniel, *Blood & Whiskey*, published in 2004. Moreover, Daniel himself is known to have pointed to Green as the man who taught him about making whiskey, and employed not just Nathan Green, but also three of Green's sons. A well-known photo of Daniel posing with his distillery hands has a Black man in it. This man is sometimes misidentified as Nathan Green, but it is actually his son George. Two of Green's descendants number among the numerous multigenerational employees of the Jack Daniel's Distillery.

The story of Nathan Green was known in Moore County and thereabouts, having long been part of local folklore, which is unsurprising given that Green's family is still living in those parts. Brown-Forman was never covering it up, as is sometimes implied. The tale of Green and Daniel was there, known and spoken of, for decades. Instead of being a secret, Green was simply not publicized as part of Brown-Forman's marketing. His place was not regularly promoted by the company and thus largely ignored by the wider world, despite having figured prominently in two separate biographies about Daniel.

Just as Green's story was overlooked for decades, the larger story of enslaved distillery workers in America continues to remain largely ignored. Putting Green in his proper context is important, as he was hardly unique. The connection between slavery and whiskey goes back at least to George Washington's whiskey distillery at Mount Vernon, which by 1799 was the largest whiskey producer in the country, with an output of over 11,000 gallons annually. This distillery was operated by six enslaved men, identified in the records as Hanson, Peter, Nat, Daniel, James, and Timothy. Mount Vernon also ran its own cooperage, with three slaves making barrels: Tom, Moses, and Jacob. Bourbon historian Mike Veach indicated that President Andrew Jackson is known to have used an enslaved distiller, because apparently that slave ran away and Jackson took out newspaper advertisements to find him.

Several of the famous names in Kentucky bourbon are antebellum figures: Elijah Craig, Evan Williams, Jacob and David Beam, William Larue Weller, and Oscar Pepper, among others. Some of them are known to have owned slaves. That none of these Kentucky bourbon distillers from the slavery era either owned or hired skilled enslaved African Americans to make their whiskey is most unlikely, but little research has been done on the subject, and what research exists has been given paltry attention by the media or the companies associated with those names.

Following the publicity of 2016 and 2017, Jack Daniel's began speaking to the Green family legacy, and the old rickhouse used to host tastings is now named in honor of George Green. A whiskey brand based in nearby Shelbyville, Uncle Nearest, expands on and enshrines that legacy. But the larger narrative remains untold, in particular the role of enslaved people in the brand histories of Kentucky bourbon. Almost a decade after Nathan Green's story first began receiving the attention it deserved, the stories of other men like Green remain stubbornly out of sight.

suppressed, the Nathan "Nearest" Green story was simply ignored by the wider world until it began appearing in the media in 2016 and 2017.

Call's distilling business was rooted in access to grain, technical knowledge and experience, and a proper water source. Lincoln County enjoyed an advantage in common with the bourbon distillers of Kentucky, in that much of the land sits on a limestone shelf. Some features of limestone springwater are useful to distilling, such as its low acidity, which encourages fermentation. Limestone filters out traces of iron from the water, and iron turns whiskey foul. This matters less today, with modern filtration tools and cheap water distillation widely available, but in the nineteenth century a sound and ready water source was vital for distilling. We don't know if Green knew about the chemistry behind it, but he certainly knew about the value of Call's springwater. It is easy to imagine Daniel, in his early days as a distillery hand, asking Green, in an impatient teenage tone, why they didn't move the distillery to that creek over yonder closer to the road, and Green explaining the importance of their spring.

The still would have been a modest affair. The typical farmer's still of that time was a copper pot with a capacity of less than a dozen gallons. It would have sat atop a crude stone furnace, and every batch of whiskey required two runs through the still. Daniel would have learned from Green the importance of making the cuts—removing the beginning and end portions from the first still run—as these contained noxious compounds. In Green's day, before gauges and other instrumentation, those cuts were made by hand, so skilled observation was crucial. The whiskey-making season ran roughly from October to June, as the summer months were too hot to ferment mash outdoors. After distilling the mash, Green would have made a point of filtering the new-make whiskey through charcoal to mellow it before storing it in barrels. This step would eventually become known as the Lincoln County Process, and it is the singular feature that separates Tennessee Whiskey from Kentucky bourbon.

## Daniel's Reconstruction

Another tall tale tucked into Jack Daniel's lapel is that the distillery was established in 1866, as the first registered distillery in the United States. Yet Daniel was barely two years into his apprenticeship in the business at that point, and he didn't have much money. The Daniel family farm was not sold until the next year, but the proceeds from the sale, including Daniel's inheritance, would be tied up in court for years to come. I subscribe to the theory that Daniel, years later, made the claim of having founded his business in 1866, knowing that an older, well-established distillery would be better received by the public.

Instead, in 1866 Daniel was busy learning the whiskey trade, and there was more to that education than making whiskey. Young Daniel was diminutive, but he had a way with people that made him a natural salesman. As Drew Hannush put it in his book *The Lost History of Tennessee Whiskey*, Daniel could get folks excited about whatever he was selling. Dan Call largely sold his whiskey through his general store, but with Daniel on the team his wares were poured into jugs and taken on the wagon roads. Daniel peddled Call's whiskey around the county at first, but eventually went farther afield, ultimately making it down to Huntsville, Alabama. That town had a growing market, the transportation advantages of the Tennessee River, a railroad link, and one more key advantage: although Lynchburg was equidistant between Nashville and Huntsville, the latter presented less formidable competition. Rebounding after the war years, Nashville would soon host the biggest whiskey companies in Tennessee.

The late 1860s were hardly a safe time to be plying the Tennessee roads with a wagonload of whiskey. In the wake of the war, the state remained lawless to a considerable extent, and racial violence against the newly freed Black population was endemic. The Ku Klux Klan was the most infamous and enduring of many terrorist groups formed in the wake of Confederate defeat and was founded just 45 miles west of Lynchburg in Pulaski, Tennessee. Other lawless groups, bearing similarities to the infamous James-Younger Gang, sprang from the ranks of disgruntled Confederate veterans.

This is also around the time when an 1871 redistricting decision cut parts of Bedford, Franklin, and Lincoln Counties away to create Moore County. The Jack Daniel's Distillery—known far and wide for using the Lincoln County Process to mellow their Tennessee Whiskey—is situated in Moore County. Thus, the Lincoln County Process came to be best associated with distilleries that were not in Lincoln County. Compounding the irony, in the 1990s Lincoln County would become home to Prichard's Distillery, which does not use the Lincoln County Process to produce its whiskey.

Jack Daniel could fairly be said to have mastered all the skills needed to prosper in the whiskey trade by the time he finally gained the key component of starting his distillery: capital. A settlement was finally reached regarding the will of Calaway Daniel in 1874, and Krass lists Jack's inheritance as $1,000. To provide some context, that same year, a congressman's annual salary was set at $5,000, a cooper in relatively wealthy Pennsylvania might make $2 a day, and a decent-sized farm in Lincoln County could sell for just a few hundred dollars. Daniel was a seasoned whiskey man in the prime of his life at 28 (or 25, depending on who you believe) with quite a hefty inheritance in hand.

Rather than take the risky step of striking out entirely on his own, Daniel bought into Dan Call's existing business in 1875, and they became partners. Daniel's capital must have helped expand production, as the company abandoned modest pot stills and adopted industrial column stills. The increased output was necessary to meet the growing thirst in the network of markets Daniel had spent years cultivating in Fayetteville, Huntsville, Tullahoma, Shelbyville, and Winchester. According to his biographers, the company of Daniel & Call soon became one of the region's middling whiskey distillers.

Daniel also bought his own farm during this period, and began dressing like the Jack Daniel of legend, with the long coat and the wide-brimmed planter's hat. The decade of work and his inheritance had carried him from struggling orphan to a man of some local prominence.

However, Call was not destined to stay in the whiskey business. The Lutheran Church's ambiguous relationship with liquor began to turn hostile, and as Call grew older, he also became more active in the church. Dan's wife, Mary, who had almost certainly brought Daniel into the family business in the first place, is said to have been agitating to get out of it. By 1877, Call leased Daniel the land the distillery was on and effectively became a silent partner. Not five years later, Call left the whiskey business entirely. As the story goes, Call said thereafter that the Lord instructed him to stop preaching the gospel or stop making whiskey. He chose the latter course, much to the regret of his descendants.

## In Business Under His Own Name

After Call's departure, Daniel set about forging what today we call his brand. At first, this meant changing up the named stenciled onto the jugs of his product to "Jack Daniel Whiskey, Lynchburg, Tenn." In fits and starts, he eventually landed on the designation that has stuck to this day: Jack Daniel's Old No. 7. Some say the reasoning behind this brilliant piece of marketing is tied to the supposed luck residing in number seven, while others say that Daniel settled on the seventh iteration of his production process for his whiskey. Another explanation holds that Daniel chose the new name in 1887.

Other origin stories for the name are variations on a theme. Green tells a story about how a Tullahoma merchant told Daniel about his chain of seven stores and the advantages of buying in bulk, and an impressed Daniel chose seven as a tribute to his success. A different story involving Tullahoma involves seven barrels that were reported lost, but were found again after the replacements had already been shipped, so the originals were marked as "Old No. 7." Yet another version tells of how seven was stamped inside the head of a honey barrel used to ship the whiskey, and the client asked for more of that No. 7.

ALL GOODS WORT
PRICE CHARGED
LEM MOTLOW
YNCHBURG,TENN
Old Time
WHISK
JACK DANIEL'S
CK Daniel's
LD MEDAL
OLD
NO.7
OLD No7
ACK DANIEL
CHBURG,TENN
ACK DANIELS
OLD NO. 7
CHBURG, TENN.

"Jack Daniel's Old No. 7. Some say the reasoning behind this brilliant piece of marketing is tied to the supposed luck residing in number seven, while others say that Daniel settled on the seventh iteration of his production process for his whiskey. Another explanation holds that Daniel chose the new name in 1887."

Lem Motlow, Daniel's nephew and successor, had his own story for the name's origin. He said it came from a misplaced batch of whiskey that matured in the barrels for an extra-long seven-year stint, so his uncle named it Jack Daniel No. 7 as an age statement. That story may conflict with how Jack Daniel released age-statement whiskeys in his day, a practice recently revived by the modern company. A saucier tale is how Daniel, a short king, lifelong bachelor, and reputed ladies' man adopted the name as a reference to one of his seven girlfriends. Brand historian Nelson Eddy dismisses that theory, but he does make a good joke about it, saying it would explain why Daniel never married: "If you call your last girlfriend Old Number Seven, that marriage ain't happening." The fable I most scoff at is that the number comes from the seven barrels that were sent to the 1904 World's Fair in St. Louis, an obvious untruth because it was already being called Old No. 7 by then.

The consensus story among experts, including biographer Peter Krass, is that Daniel was infuriated when the state of Tennessee changed his distillery registration number from 7 to 16 as part of a tax district reorganization. Adding insult to injury, his was the only number so changed. That registration number was required to be on the label, so he adopted "Old No. 7" as the major labeling to put a stop to any confusion. But any certainty as to why Jack Daniel chose to label his whiskey Old No. 7 is lost to history.

While Daniel wrestled with brand development, the distilling industry in Moore County underwent a period of consolidation. Dan Call wasn't the only man getting out of the business. By the beginning of 1888, the number of distilleries in the region had shrunk to just three, with Daniel's company still occupying the middle slot. The closures prompted Daniel to leave the Call location behind, and in June 1884 he acquired the Cave Spring Hollow property where the Jack Daniel's Distillery has been ever since.

By the mid-to-late 1880s, Daniel was in his 40s and had established something of a local empire in Lynchburg. His rivals had fallen by the wayside, so he could be fairly described as the last man standing in the Moore County whiskey business. His main competition was now in Nashville, either in the form of Nashville-based distillers like Nelson's Greenbrier or Nashville-owned enterprises like Tullahoma's Cascade Hollow. So, Daniel set his sights on invading the Nashville market. He would do this through producing quality, not quantity, and capped production at 300 gallons of whiskey per day. Even with that success, the Tennessee of the time was a relative minnow in the national whiskey industry, with an output much, much smaller than giants like Illinois, Kentucky, and Pennsylvania.

Daniel began bottling his whiskey following changes in the market and technology. In previous decades, glass bottles were handblown, and handicrafts do not come cheap. Although George Garvin Brown began bottling Old Forester in Louisville, Kentucky, in 1870, few whiskey companies copied his practice in the years that followed, at least not until bottles could be mass produced. Although he was known to bottle his own limited-release whiskeys for expositions and the like, it wasn't until 1895 that Jack Daniel made the switch from jugs and barrels to bottles. In so doing, he put another stamp on the classic look of Jack Daniel's Old No. 7.

The modern story behind the square, clear glass bottle is twofold. The practical version is the squared shape was chosen because it was more stable in the packaging and shipping of the day. The colorful version is that it was the last design shown to Daniel, who chose it on impulse, saying, "A square bottle for a square shooter." Either way, Daniel laid the cornerstone for his brand at a pivotal time. The late nineteenth century is when many of the brands that form the backbone of our everyday life came into being: Campbell's Soup, Arm & Hammer Baking Soda, Nabisco Crackers, Oscar Mayer, Keebler Cookies, Levi-Strauss, Heinz Ketchup, and Coca-Cola were all being sold by the time Daniel's squared glass bottles came into being.

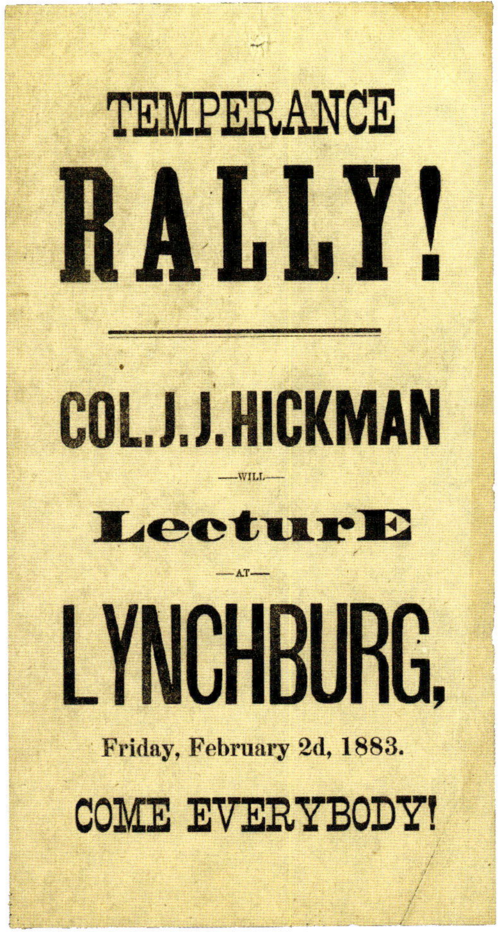


The dawn of the twentieth century put Daniel well into his 50s. Mr. Daniel was a man of means who indulged in a rich Southern diet; today we would say he was not taking care of himself. Although the temperance movement had annoyed him throughout his career, it was gaining momentum. In his native Tennessee, "the Dries" were enjoying success at the statehouse, chipping away at where liquor could be sold in the state, with more than half the counties in the Volunteer State living under some form of Prohibition.

His declining energy showed when Daniel set off to St. Louis' 1904 World's Fair to give his whiskey one last big push. As it is told, everyone from still hands to local politicians to his nephew and heir Lem Motlow had to encourage him to pack himself up and get to St. Louis. He may have just been having fun with them all, feigning reluctance, but the younger Jack Daniel who plied the wagon roads would have been sorting out the shipping before even the first suggestion reached his ears.

The 1904 World's Fair, also known as The Louisiana Purchase Exposition, would come to rival the 1893 Chicago World's Fair in terms of its fame, scope, and legacy. The sprawling event lasted from the end of April to the beginning of December that year. The 1904 Summer Olympics ran concurrently with the World's Fair in St. Louis late that summer, subsumed into the larger exposition.

Many more folks than Jack Daniel came to St. Louis looking to showcase their wares. If you believe all the popular stories about the 1904 World's Fair,

JACK DAN
DISTILLERY
NO.
1
EST. 1866
LYNCHBURG, T

foods as quintessentially American as cotton candy, peanut butter, Jello, the hamburger, and the hot dog were all introduced to the country at large at that World's Fair. Much debunking has gone into some of those claims (a version of the hamburger has been with us since at least Roman times), but I chose my wording there carefully. People traveled from far and wide to the World's Fair, and this was not the homogenized America of today, with a McDonald's and a Subway serving as mile markers on the highway. That which was not unveiled for the very first time at the Louisiana Purchase Exposition, like the hamburger, could still have been novel to a sizable number of folks in attendance.

Jack Daniel famously won the whiskey competition at the 1904 World's Fair, taking away the gold medal. As at modern spirits competitions, that was *a* gold medal and not *the* gold medal. Bushmills won a gold medal as well. Yet it is important to remember that Daniel was an underdog and outsider at this event. Tennessee was not America's number two whiskey state in 1904, as it has been since the mid-twentieth century. It ranked more like fifth or sixth. So, what Daniel did was akin to a little-known craft distiller from, say, Arizona coming into a major international spirits competition today and walking away with Best in Show.

With that achievement won, I imagine Daniel soon took stock of his declining energy, if not his health, and began looking toward retirement. There is no singular answer as to why Daniel stepped away from the business he had spent every day since he was a teenager building up, but he could see the growing power of the Dries in Tennessee and understood the threat they posed to his distillery. Daniel had always eschewed politics, and therefore likely had no appetite for a head-on battle with the temperance movement. He could also recall the prolonged court squabble that held up his own inheritance, and perhaps thought it better to settle matters while he was still alive. According to Krass, on April 16, 1907, he deeded the distillery plus 200 acres of land to two of his nephews, Lem Motlow and Dick Daniel, with the transfer to be effective on January 1, 1908. Motlow bought out his cousin's share, becoming the sole heir.

Even at the end, Daniel had room enough left in his life for one more slate of tall tales: that of his passing. The story goes that Daniel couldn't open his safe one day, gave the thing a swift kick that broke his toe, the toe became infected, and that infection took his life on October 9, 1911. The version I first heard was gruesome—that the foot turned gangrenous and had to be amputated. That never sat well with me; medical statistics from the Civil War indicate that a foot amputation was a very survivable procedure, even in the era before antibiotics. Moreover, by 1911, germ theory was widely accepted. Regardless, Daniel later had to have his leg amputated because of the injury. In what must have been a miserable stretch of several months, he endured repeated surgeries and then died.

A modern theory is that Daniel was diabetic. He was an older man, one made quite fat by a Southern diet, as well as one who liked a good drink. Nowadays we know diabetes follows hard on the heels of a lifestyle of that description. The proposal that diabetes could have compounded Daniel's recovery from surgery is a logical one. Yet some have taken this a step further and given the tale a modern twist. Some critics had already asserted long ago that kicking the safe was just a fable and Daniel contracted the infection in some other way. So, following from the diabetic theory, it has been put forward that it was never an infection at all, and that diabetes took Daniel's foot and then leg. This is the internet age; diabetes claiming feet and legs is a fixture of modern life, and new stories spread rapidly. However, this example of modern myth-making is as much about Jack Daniel's capacity to capture the modern imagination as it is about the internet as a font of misinformation.

Kicking the safe is the official version, though. Nelson Eddy's opinion is that Daniel was done in, like President James A. Garfield, by too much inept medical attention. Daniel was already in failing health, and the painful treatments and operations were too much for him. As for the ideas that kicking the safe was not involved or that Daniel's death was not even connected to infection, Eddy maintains that the safe, broken toe, and resulting gangrene is how the story has always been told, since even before Daniel died.

"Even at the end, Daniel had room enough left in his life for one more slate of tall tales: that of his passing. The story goes that Daniel couldn't open his safe one day, gave the thing a swift kick that broke his toe, the toe became infected, and that infection took his life on October 9, 1911."

# Bill Hughes

Officially, the first Master Distiller at the Jack Daniel's Distillery was Mr. Jack himself. Yet Jack Daniel wore many hats in his whiskey business—marketing director, sales manager, and distillery boss to name just a few—and whiskey was not his only business concern. When it came to running the daily operation of the distillery, Daniel had help in the form of Bill Hughes.

Bill was the son of Colonel John Mason Hughes, one of the major distillers in the Lynchburg area in the post-Civil War era. Colonel Hughes was partners with Jack Eaton, son of Alfred Eaton, the distiller who brought the Lincoln County Process to Lincoln County. Alfred Eaton's distillery was also the first to use Cave Spring, so Jack Eaton was as close to Lynchburg whiskey-making royalty as it got in those days. Another partner of Hughes's was Ben Tolley, whose family were also prominent distillers. Collectively, Hughes, Eaton, and Tolley formed something of a Lynchburg whiskey-making combine. Dan Call was affiliated with that combine, which is how Jack Daniel came to do some transportation and sales work for Hughes.

The whiskey business around Lynchburg then was a small world where everyone knew each other, and this time was when some of the families who have enjoyed multigenerational employment at the Jack Daniel's Distillery got their start. Ben A. Green wrote that Daniel working for Colonel Hughes came back around when Daniel hired Bill in 1885. According to Peter Krass, Bill Hughes had received some education at a private military academy, so Daniel charged him with the company bookkeeping. Within two years, Hughes had risen to become Daniel's distillery manager. The exact date is unknown, but whiskey historian Drew Hannush believes it was after Nathan Green left the scene.

Perhaps more important to the future of the company than working as Daniel's deputy and plant manager, Hughes also played mentor to Lem Motlow. When Motlow turned 18 and was hired by his Uncle Jack, he moved in with Hughes, who was living in a small house on the distillery property. Motlow evolved from roommate into de facto boarder after Hughes was married, only moving out after the birth of Hughes's first child.

No matter what date one selects as the starting point of Jack Daniel's Distillery, Jack was undoubtedly the first man in charge of making his own whiskey. But when the notion is framed as Daniel in sole ownership of his own company *and* having it located in Cave Spring Hollow, the man making the whiskey was Bill Hughes. What is more, job titles like "master distiller," "head distiller," and "distillery manager" are often interchangeable, even today. Jack Daniel's itself did not formally adopt the job title of Master Distiller until the 1990s, and the men who are now known as their past Master Distillers had titles like head distiller or distillery manager.

For their limited-edition series The Master Distillers, Jack Daniel's chose to skip Bill Hughes, naming Mr. Jack as the first and Jess Motlow as the second. Although a case could be made for putting Hughes in between them, he doesn't fit cleanly into the official narrative that has Jack Daniel as founder, owner, operator, and creator-in-chief. Also, no members of the Hughes or Eaton families are known to be among the distillery's workforce today. So, Bill Hughes may never have been the Master Distiller of Jack Daniel's, but he was certainly the first distillery manager at Cave Spring Hollow, and deserves his nod accordingly.

# Cave Spring's Camillus

Lem Motlow took charge from Jack Daniel in 1908, entering in the midst of a losing battle against the fast-rising floodwaters of the temperance movement. He was experienced and well-prepared to run the business, but it was his temperament that made him ideally suited for the struggle to preserve Jack Daniel's and make Tennessee safe for producing whiskey again.

When a young Calaway Daniel and his family arrived in Middle Tennessee, around the time of the War of 1812, there were already Motlows living in the frontier region that would come to host Lynchburg. Jack became tied to the family when his sister Finetta married Felix Motlow, a union that produced Lemuel in 1869. Lem followed very much in his uncle's footsteps, working on Daniel's farm as a teen, just as Daniel himself had done for first his father and then Dan Call.

The young Motlow had to wait a little longer than his uncle to begin working as a whiskey man, not taking his first steps until he was 18. Motlow was given his first distillery task in 1887, making sugar maple charcoal. But that first step was accompanied by moving in with Bill Hughes, who was certainly Jack Daniel's head distiller, if not actually the "Master Distiller." Short of Nathan Green or Jack himself, it's hard to imagine who could have given Motlow a better grounding in the craft of whiskey making than Hughes.

Lem Motlow was hardly the only Daniel relation that came into Daniel's business, and wasn't even the only Motlow. According to Peter Krass, when the squared bottles were introduced, it was Lem's brother Tim who was hired to do the bottling and boxing of those bottles. But it was Lem who mirrored his uncle best in his ambition, business acumen, and determination. Before taking the reins at the distillery, Ben A. Green wrote that Motlow was already an accomplished mule trader, owner of several saloons, had accumulated substantial farm properties, gotten into banking, and had started and partnered his own liquor-making businesses.

Yet beyond their similar drives to succeed in business, the two men could not have been more different. Daniel was gregarious, stylish, and ingratiating. Motlow was sullen, often plainly dressed, hot-tempered, and pugnacious. The restless Motlow had challenged his uncle's production cap at the distillery, which limited whiskey output as a quality-control measure. A young man in a hurry, Motlow had no patience for that.

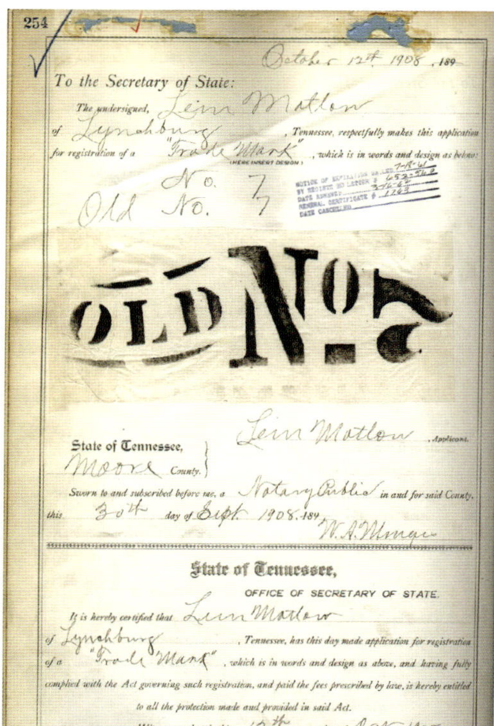

254

October 12th 1908, 189

To the Secretary of State:

The undersigned, Lem Motlow of Lynchburg, Tennessee, respectfully makes this application for registration of a "Trade Mark" (HERE INSERT DESIGN), which is in words and design as below:

Old No. 7

OLD No. 7

Lem Motlow, Applicant.

State of Tennessee, Moore County.

Sworn to and subscribed before me, a Notary Public in and for said County, this 30th day of Sept. 1908. W. A. Morgan

State of Tennessee,

OFFICE OF SECRETARY OF STATE.

It is hereby certified that Lem Motlow of Lynchburg, Tennessee, has this day made application for registration of a "Trade Mark", which is in words and design as above, and having fully complied with the Act governing such registration, and paid the fees prescribed by law, is hereby entitled to all the protection made and provided in said Act.

Witness my hand, this 12th day of Oct 1908.

As you can guess, Daniel frequently clashed with his nephew.

Another thing that made Motlow and Daniel two very different people was their family life. Daniel was famously a bachelor to the end of his days, but Motlow married twice. With his first wife, Clara Reagor, he had a son, John Reagor Motlow. But Clara died in 1901, and he remarried to Ophelia Evans in 1903. With Ophelia, Lem Motlow had three more sons and a daughter.

Regarding one distinction between the two, Motlow clearly had the upper hand: he wanted to engage in state politics and fight back against the temperance movement. For Daniel, politics was anathema, and as dismayed as he was by the growing power of the Dries in Tennessee, he did nothing to oppose them. Historians of Prohibition generally agree that brewers and distillers in America underestimated the power of the temperance movement, particularly how it became the unlikely nexus of two powerful forces in early twentieth century American politics: nativists—who identified drink with immigrants from Germany, Ireland, and Italy—and suffragettes, who blamed alcohol as the driving force behind domestic violence and numerous other social ills affecting women. The combative Motlow wanted to enter the arena and do battle with these threats to his enterprises; Daniel, especially at the end of his life, found it all unappealing.

Only a year after Motlow took over the Daniel whiskey business in Lynchburg, the state government enacted Prohibition in two stages. The first bill to pass the state senate in 1909 made it a crime to sell or consume alcohol within four miles of a school. A second bill passed later that year banned the manufacture of any alcoholic beverages in the state. The governor, Malcolm Patterson, vetoed both bills, but those vetoes were overridden by a supermajority in the legislature.

The liquor ban in Tennessee was hugely popular in rural areas, but not so much in the state's leading cities. Hillary Howse and Edward "Boss" Crump, the mayors of Nashville and Memphis respectively, openly ignored the anti-liquor laws. This defiance prompted the dry supermajority in the statehouse to pass the "Ouster Law" in 1915, which provided the means to remove any public official who refused to enforce state laws. Crump left office before he could be forced out in court, while Howse resigned under a cloud of corruption (he eventually returned to the mayor's office in 1923). Even without those men in office, both cities remained notoriously soaked with booze throughout the Prohibition years.

Motlow responded by shuttering the distillery, while taking his business to familiar territory in Alabama. His older brother, Frank "Spoon" Motlow, had spearheaded the opening of saloons and distilleries in Gadsden and

# Jack Daniel's Is Still in a Dry County

Lem Motlow scored a litany of political and business victories in his lifetime. What Lem Motlow, nor any of his descendants, would not win back was the right to sell liquor on the Motlow home turf. Moore County remained dry for decades, with visitors to the Jack Daniel's Distillery unable to try or buy any of the whiskey that drew them to the place while on-site.

Under Tennessee law, restrictions on liquor are decided on a county-by-county basis, by the voters in that county. Recall that the powers that be in Lynchburg resisted Lem Motlow's efforts to legalize the restoration of the Jack Daniel's Distillery, and he won the right to restore the Jack Daniel's Distillery by a thin margin. the Temperance movement continued to have a strong presence in rural Tennessee long after Prohibition was finished as a national force and remains influential in the area to this day. Jack Daniel's even had a teetotaler Master Distiller, Jess Gamble, in the mid-1960s. Moore County residents continue to have a complex relationship with their region's most important employer and major source of fame and pride. "There's always been that tension at the local level," said historian Nelson Eddy, speaking of the dynamic between the distillery and the Dries.

Moore County residents were persuaded in 1995 to loosen liquor sales restrictions, permitting the distillery to sell bottlings of a commemorative nature. Technically, that makes it a "moist" county rather than a dry one, even if restrictions are tighter than is usually the case for a moist jurisdiction. Typically, a moist county legalizes the sale of beer and wine at restaurants. In the case of Jack Daniel's, an exception was made so the distillery could sell bottles at the distillery gift shop.

That loophole opened for Jack Daniel's was later exploited by others. Anyone who walks around the Lynchburg town square will spy Lynchburg Winery. This outfit does tastings and sells bottles, just as the distillery does, and wine. The town also has a craft-level distillery in operation, Lynchburg Distillery, that exploits the loophole.

Leaving these exceptions aside, Moore County is still almost dry. The area lacks liquor stores, has no bars, and only some of the local eateries sell beer. Locals clearly prefer it that way, as there is no clamor to throw the doors open on liquor sales in general, and it is not hard to understand why. One can only imagine that Lynchburg's quaint town square would lose most of its charm if every other storefront became a bar, which would inevitably happen if regular retail liquor sales were legalized.

Another issue local people have with what is by far their largest business entity is whiskey fungus. A common sight wherever spirits are barrel aged, the black (nontoxic) fungus feeds on the alcohol vapor evaporating from the barrels of stored liquor. The fungus is a common sight wherever spirits are matured around the world, and in the vicinity of Jack Daniel's sprawling rickhouse complexes (95 rickhouses storing more than 2 million barrels), the black fungus can be found on buildings, trees, furniture, and even vehicles. The problem locals have with it is the fungus doesn't respect property boundaries and grows on their homes. Christi Long, a resident of neighboring Lincoln County, filed a lawsuit against Jack Daniel's, complaining that she spent $10,000 annually on power washing her events venue business. In 2023, a judge found that one rickhouse under construction lacked proper permits and ordered a halt to work there. But Long's aim was to force Brown-Forman to clear out all of the neighboring rickhouses, and that the judge refused to do. Lawsuits of this type are often dismissed in Tennessee, but it does indicate that not everyone in the area loves Jack Daniel's and what they do. That ambivalence ensures that Moore County will remain almost arid for the foreseeable future.

Birmingham, with his brothers acting as more or less silent partners. Alabama offered only a short-term haven, however. The temperance movement there was almost as potent as in the Volunteer State, with Gadsden going dry (and consequently closing that branch of the Motlow liquor empire) in 1908. Birmingham also went dry in a county-wide measure that was repealed in 1911, and then dry again when Alabama enacted its own statewide Prohibition in 1915. Statewide Prohibition in Alabama would outlive national Prohibition, lasting until 1937.

Jack Daniel's whiskey had one remaining refuge that was, for a while, outside the grasp of the Dries: St. Louis, Missouri. Jack Daniel's historian Nelson Eddy believes the reason Motlow looked to St. Louis was because he had business ties there going back to Jack Daniel's gold medal–winning appearance at the 1904 World's Fair.

Motlow set up shop in a two-story brick building at 3960 Duncan Avenue and made Jack Daniel's whiskey there for the next several years. Although no longer made in Tennessee and certainly not with Cave Spring water, it was produced using the same techniques as in Lynchburg, including the sugar maple charcoal mellowing. Motlow even went to the trouble of bringing some Green family men to work at the St. Louis distillery. Ironically, at least some of that production was quietly shipped back home to Tennessee by mail, since the law only made it illegal to consume drink within four miles of a school. If you could get it, drinking it anywhere not so excluded was still permitted.

Shortly after the move to St. Louis, US Secretary of War Jacob Dickinson introduced President Taft to Jack Daniel's, which we know because of a surviving letter from Taft thanking the civilian chief of the US Army for a gift of some of the whiskey. Since the letter is dated from 1911, the whiskey was undoubtedly produced during the Lynchburg era.

In 1917, a bipartisan majority passed the Eighteenth Amendment to the Constitution, which banned the sale and production of alcoholic beverages. President Woodrow Wilson promptly signed the amendment. Approval of the measure by the states was a trickle through 1918, but then suddenly came an avalanche of over two dozen ratifications in January 1919. Tennessee, which had been ardently dry for a decade, was one of the states that waited a year before joining the drinkless party; it ratified to approve the Eighteenth Amendment on January 13.

In the aftermath of the First World War, Lem Motlow found himself out of the whiskey business. Or rather, out of the legitimate whiskey business. As for his outpost in St. Louis, that oft-forgotten one-time home of Jack Daniel's on Duncan Avenue stood until 2005, when the building was demolished. Today the address sits inside the sprawling site of the St. Louis IKEA.

"As for his outpost in St. Louis, that oft-forgotten one-time home of Jack Daniel's on Duncan Avenue stood until 2005, when the building was demolished. Today the address sits inside the sprawling site of the St. Louis IKEA."

# Jess Motlow

Born in 1876, Jesse Butler Motlow was the third son of Felix Motlow and Jack Daniel's sister, Nettie Josephine Daniel. Like his older brother Lem as well as Bill Hughes, Jess Motlow was taught whiskey making by Jack Daniel. It was with Daniel's retirement that the role of Master Distiller emerged clearly in Lynchburg. Lem's talents were principally in business, and he was the owner. Mr. Jack appointed Jess Motlow into the role of actually making the Old No. 7 whiskey.

Prohibition would hamstring Jess's career in making whiskey even more than it did his older brother Lem, seeing as how no one has ever alleged that Jesse participated in bootlegging. Yet like Lem, Jess was one of a few that was at Jack Daniel's both before and after Prohibition, and he was at least as instrumental as his brother in the distillery's revival. If Lem's foresight, tenacity, stamina, and resources were the foundation upon which Jack Daniel's was rebuilt, Jess had the knowledge, earned through his apprenticeship with his uncle and hands-on, day-to-day labor. "If Jess hadn't been there, there would be no Jack Daniel's," said one of his successors as Master Distiller, Jeff Arnett.

Officially, Jess retired in 1941. One imagines that having done his part to rebuild the distillery, work the kinks out of the new equipment, and train his successors, he was not inclined to stay on past retirement age. Even if he did not need it, Social Security was looking stable and successful, having issued its first monthly benefit check just the year before.

Even so, Jess Motlow was one of those outsized characters that the American whiskey trade seemed to attract in droves. He was known for wearing extra-baggy trousers, and it is said his reason for doing so was to tuck away pint bottles of whiskey for consumption during the day. Much as Jimmy Russell has done at Wild Turkey today, Jess continued as a presence at the distillery even after his successor took the helm, so his "retirement" was relative. I've seen a late-1940s era picture of Jess and his nephew Reagor Motlow inspecting a wagon of corn, and he was around to figure prominently in the famous 1951 *Fortune* magazine article that helped bring Jack Daniel's into the spotlight. In that article, Reagor was quoted as saying, "Uncle Jess here never read a chemistry text in his life, but after fifty-four years of stillin' whiskey you can't fool his eye, his nose, or his tongue."

Jess Motlow lived just long enough to see the sale of the family distillery to Brown-Forman, securing its future, albeit not as one owned and operated by *his* family. Jess passed away in October 1957 and is buried not far from his brother Lem and uncle Jack in Lynchburg's town cemetery.

## A Dark Decade for Motlow

Although whiskey would remain Lem Motlow's passion project for the rest of his life, he had other businesses to fall back on when his distillery was shuttered. For example, although the automotive industry as we know it today was born in 1908 with the Ford Model T, Krass reports that Motlow's mule-trading business was still quite lucrative in 1920. He was already a millionaire in 1920, with a fortune worth approximately $50 million in today's money.

Among his assets was a substantial stockpile of whiskey. Congress passed the Volstead Act, enabling the provisions of the Eighteenth Amendment as enforceable law, later in 1919. President Wilson vetoed the measure, but he was overridden by a bipartisan majority in Congress. The federal government was authorized to issue licenses to produce and sell medicinal spirits, as spirits were very much considered proper medicine in those days. Six companies were so licensed, and Lem Motlow's was not among them. So almost a thousand barrels of whiskey sat under guard in St. Louis, and Motlow had few legal avenues for selling them.

The first incident came in December 1922, when three men, masked and armed, appeared at the Duncan Avenue warehouse. As related by the *St. Louis Post-Dispatch*, they forced the guards into the basement and made off with 118 cases of bottled whiskey and 16 barrels. It is believed that Egan's Rats, a predominately (but not exclusively) Irish American gang that had a powerful presence in the St. Louis underworld, were responsible. Egan's Rats wouldn't trouble Jack Daniel's again, however, as the robbery came only a short time before the gang was broken up by law enforcement: in 1924, an imprisoned member squealed on the crew's leadership, sending nine leaders of the gang to prison.

Motlow's next brush with criminals would come shortly after the robbery, the following summer, when his whiskey caught the attention of would-be bootleggers in St. Louis. These were neophytes to the fast-evolving world of booze and crime in the Prohibition era, however, so they brought in an expert: George Remus, the infamous "King of the Bootleggers." As detailed in Karen Abbott's *The Ghosts of Eden Park*, Remus, only recently released from a stint in a federal prison in Atlanta, was leery of becoming engaged in a large venture—especially anything involving partners he did not know well and could not control. He was eventually persuaded by a former partner, John Marcus, to become involved in the caper.

The deal was that Remus and his partners, under the guise of a dummy corporation, would buy the Jack Daniel's stockpile and its associated paperwork for $125,000. The contracts for this transaction were signed in June 1923. Motlow got paid, and the whiskey remained under government supervision at the Duncan Avenue warehouse. One of the inspectors assigned to that warehouse was William J. Kinney, who got the job through political patronage. Kinney was an associate of Egan's Rats, and a conspirator in the bootlegging scheme.

While Kinney looked the other way, the bootleggers siphoned off whiskey from the barrels, using hoses to feed it onto trucks waiting outside the warehouse. Remus told his new partners to drain six gallons from each of the 40-gallon barrels, so that when they were refilled with water and neutral alcohol, the tampering would go undetected. According to Doria Lynch, writing for the US District Court, Southern District of Indiana (where the case would ultimately be tried), that plan would have netted the bootleggers 5,000 gallons of whiskey.

However, the King's new partners were greedy and ignored his instructions. Over a couple of weeks in August, they stole six times more whiskey than he'd recommended. The whiskey in the refilled barrels could in no way fool any inspector who bothered to actually taste it. Their plan was to rely on Kinney and other bribed staff to make sure any gaugers outside their control only got to assess undisturbed barrels. This ill-considered plan collapsed as soon as a gauger arrived when none of the conspirators were at the warehouse. With one sip, the entire plot unraveled.

The first barrels of stolen Jack Daniel's whiskey were seized, along with John Marcus, just west of Indianapolis, which is why the criminal case wound up in an Indiana courtroom. The change of venue suited prosecutors, who didn't think they could get a conviction in St. Louis, not with the prominent businessmen and politicians they were planning to indict as part of Remus's ring. They weren't wrong: when the St. Louis defendants departed by train for their trial, a crowd of 4,000 supporters saw them off from the station. Indiana, on the other hand, was as fervently dry a state as Tennessee. Lem Motlow was among the 31 people charged in the case.

On March 17, 1924, Motlow made a court appearance in St. Louis, then went out for dinner and drinks with friends before boarding the Louisville & Nashville train back to Tennessee. Motlow was in his middle 50s by now and was tired and at least a little drunk that night. On the way to his sleeper compartment, he was stopped for his ticket by the porter, Ed Wallis, who was Black. Motlow, still quarrelsome despite middle age, was aghast at being hindered by Wallis. The two argued, which brought the conductor, Clarence Pullis, to the scene. Pullis was white. According to the *St. Louis Post-Dispatch*, a scuffle quickly ensued, before the train had even left the city. Motlow was armed, and shot Pullis, who died of his wounds two days later.

# Jack and Coke Go Together Better than You Think

Jack Daniel's and Coca-Cola is one of the classic combos in the drinks world, if not *the* classic. When it comes to mixing a spirit with Coke specifically, the only peer is the Cuba Libre, or rum and Coke, and for that one the rum chosen doesn't matter. As for mixing soft drinks with other whiskeys, I once had a neighbor in Washington, DC, who was passionately committed to Evan Williams and RC Cola, and many Kentuckians are partial to their choice of bourbon and our local soft drink, Ale-8-One. Those are all personal preferences or else pegged to a particular soft drink. The underlying message is that no other specific combination of Spiritous Liquor A plus Soft Drink B has risen to this level of popular identification and bar staple as the ubiquitous Jack and Coke.

The two are so ubiquitous that Jack and Coke are a canned, ready-to-drink (RTD) cocktail (with a decent 7% ABV at that), underlining that both brands recognize the power of their connection. The calorie conscious can even buy a Coke Zero version of the drink. Visitors to the Jack Daniel's Distillery in Lynchburg can order frozen Jack and Coke at the visitor center, a move I strongly recommend during the steamy summer months.

Yet there is a little more of a story behind the exemplary compatibility of these two world-famous, industry-leading brands—Coca-Cola sits on a distant branch of the Motlow family tree.

Lem and Jess Motlow's great-great-grandparents were Obediah Hooper and Massilva Marvula Brooks. Another distant descendant of that union is Asa Griggs Candler. Born in 1851, Candler was Lem Motlow's third cousin. In terms of age, he was older than Lem, but younger than Jack Daniel himself, and Daniel is not a blood relation of Candler's.

Candler bought a soft drink formula from a chemist named John Pemberton in 1888. A few years later, he started a company to produce and sell that soft drink, naming his business the Coca-Cola Company.

There is no evidence the two men ever met, and therefore they probably did not. It is hard to imagine that the marketers working for these companies would not surface the story if there was even the barest possibility of Motlow and Candler having crossed paths. Also, neither man actually invented their respective famous drinks. Yet neither Coca-Cola nor Jack Daniel's, two of the world's most famous and best-selling drinks brands—one soft and one hard—would exist today without them. The two have some story elements in common, in addition to sharing a little DNA.

JACK DANIEL'S
OLD
No. 7
BRAND
TENNESSEE WHISKEY
MIXED WITH
Coca-Cola
Alc. 5% Vol. 330ml

JACK &

Lem Motlow was promptly arrested and charged with murder. As ugly as the crime was, the trial was equally as sordid. Drawing on his substantial resources, Motlow hired a dream team of high-powered St. Louis attorneys, led by Patrick Cullen. At the trial in December 1924, the sitting governor of Tennessee, Austin Peay, appeared as a character witness for the defendant.

Motlow took the stand and claimed he was attacked by Wallis and that he accidentally shot Pullis, who had grabbed him from behind. Wallis testified that when Pullis appeared, Motlow demanded of him, "Where did you get that black [epithet deleted]?" shoved Wallis back, drew his pistol, and began firing.

However, Motlow's defense was not based on testimony pertaining to his character or even an assertion of self-defense. Instead, his lawyers demeaned the surviving victim of that night, Wallis, with racist slurs and innuendo. On cross-examination, defense attorneys asked Wallis if he belonged to any civil rights groups. The implication that he was engaged as such, in segregated America, would have inflamed the all-white jury. They mocked Wallis for the way he spoke, and court records show that the defense repeatedly referred to Wallis using racial epithets throughout the trial.

In closing arguments, defense attorney Frank Bond asserted, "There are two kinds of [epithet deleted] in the South. There are those who know their place ... and those who have ambitions for racial equality. In such a class falls Wallis, the race reformer, the man who would be socially equal to you all, gentlemen of the jury." On December 10, the jury acquitted Motlow. "We did not believe the negro," said jury foreman Frederick Smith. Jurors actually shook hands with Motlow outside the courthouse.

Motlow got away with murder in a way that was typical of powerful, wealthy white men under Jim Crow, and the mid-1920s were arguably the height of that era. The KKK would infamously parade down Pennsylvania Avenue in 1925, numbering over 30,000 strong. Yet the times only underscore what is, in my opinion, the ugliest tale in American whiskey lore, and the incident severely taints the legacy of the man who would go on to revive Jack Daniel's Tennessee Whiskey. According to Krass, Motlow's descendants spoke so little of the incident that one of his grandchildren didn't learn of it until adulthood, and then only from someone outside the family.

Yet Motlow went on with his life, and because of the culture of that time, continued on nearly unscathed. First, he never had to journey to Indiana and face trial with the rest of the defendants in the St. Louis bootlegging case. A week before that trial began, Motlow arranged to have his case separated from the rest of the defendants. He didn't go to court on his bootlegging charges until

1926, and when he did, the trial was held in the US District Court of Middle Tennessee. Unsurprisingly, the judge found the case against Motlow unpersuasive and dismissed the charges.

During the late 1920s, Motlow sold the last remnants of the St. Louis stock of Jack Daniel's whiskey to Schenley Industries in New York, one of the companies licensed to deal in medicinal whiskey. The company was run by Lewis Rosenstiel, a man who would later earn the sobriquet "The Bad Boy of Bourbon."

Rosenstiel had wished to use the Jack Daniel's Old No. 7 label for bottling the stock he acquired from Motlow, but Motlow insisted on receiving a fee for the use of that trademark. He had been careful to keep the Jack Daniel's brand in regular use with his other enterprises after the arrival of Prohibition, retaining a firm grip on its ownership. Rosenstiel's lawyers figured a way around this by releasing it as Jack Daniel Old No. 8, and this slight shift was enough to pass muster with intellectual property law in the early twentieth century. While Rosenstiel claimed this little victory, he would later discover that pugnacity ran in the Motlow blood, and the family never forgot anyone who crossed them.

One last bit of bad luck befell the legacy of Jack Daniel before the decade was out. In 1927, a flour fire burned down much of the original Jack Daniel's Distillery in Cave Spring Hollow. By New Year's Eve 1929, Wall Street had crashed, the Great Depression was just starting to unfold, and many of the physical vestiges of what had been Jack Daniel's Tennessee Whiskey were gone.

## Revival

A decade of Prohibition had revealed that America's greatest experiment in social engineering was, in many ways, a disaster. As the libertarian think tank the Cato Institute would write of Prohibition, "[It] was undertaken to reduce crime and corruption, solve social problems, reduce the tax burden created by prisons and poorhouses, and improve health and hygiene in America. The results of that experiment clearly indicate that it was a miserable failure on all counts." The most ardent temperance advocates would not admit it, of course, but everyone else could see that Prohibition was a shambles.

The Great Depression, Prohibition, and many other ails had Americans desperate for change by the early 1930s. People everywhere were reconsidering many of their old ideas about how things ought to be. Going into the 1932 election, "Sunny Jim" Watson, the Republican Senate Majority Leader, said of the national attitude towards his party, "We are all going into the ash heap together." The Democratic Party won by a landslide, ushering in the first term of President Franklin Delano Roosevelt and a wide Democratic majority in Congress. It was the start of the famous New Deal, and part of that New Deal was the repeal of Prohibition.

The proposed Twenty-First Amendment, which would effectively cancel the Eighteenth Amendment, passed Congress before Roosevelt was even sworn in. Yet the Dries were strongly entrenched in statehouses around the country. Proponents of the repeal feared it would never be ratified by the necessary three-fourths of state governments if the usual means of passing an amendment were used, even though Prohibition's repeal was an issue in the landslide Democratic victory. So, they resorted to using state ratifying conventions, specifically formed to bypass those dug-in opponents.

So, even though Tennessee was the nineteenth state to ratify the repeal of Prohibition, Lem Motlow still faced an uphill struggle to make that appeal mean anything to him and his prospects. The Twenty-First Amendment did nothing to affect state-level Prohibition, so Motlow ran for the Tennessee House of Representatives to take on the Dries in person. Proving that the scandals of the 1920s had done no harm to his reputation, Motlow won the election and served from 1933 to 1937. He then ran for state senator and held that office from 1939 to 1941.

From the statehouse, Motlow helped repeal the ban on liquor production in Tennessee in 1937. An indication of just how strong Dry forces were in the state is that the repeal ban initially allowed for only the manufacture of liquor; selling it in Tennessee was still banned. Moreover, this production could only be done if the county to host said liquor business also repealed the ban on its local level.

In Motlow's next move, he asked the Moore County Court to call for a referendum on repealing the local ban. They refused, forcing Motlow to appeal to the state supreme court. They sided with Motlow, ordering Moore County to hold the vote. Motlow was assailed by local newspapers and from the county's pulpits, but he won that vote by a narrow majority. The way was open for Jack Daniel's whiskey to be made by Cave Spring Hollow for the first time in more than three-and-a-half decades.

Motlow recalled as many old still hands as he could, erected a new brick distillery, and filled his first barrel on November 11, 1938. By contrast, James Beauregard Beam, who also had to start over in the whiskey business from scratch, had his first post-Repeal batch in the barrel in 1935. Those three years of fighting it out in the halls of the state capitol, in court, and at the ballot box underscore one key difference between being a Kentucky bourbon baron and making whiskey on the edge of Tennessee's Highland Rim.

The reborn Jack Daniel's was a self-financed project, and Motlow felt the urgency familiar to most craft distilling start-ups today: the need to get a product on the market and generate some revenue. Yet he had not gone to the trouble of carefully preserving his uncle's brand name only to cheapen its value by putting that name on an immature whiskey. One year after the revival, the company put Lem Motlow's Sour Mash Whiskey on the market. The brand continued on for decades as a younger, cheaper version of Old No. 7 before being discontinued in 1990.

Proper maturation held that the flagship whiskey would need to sit in the barrels for a few more years, and by then the United States had entered the Second World War.

Having been in poor health for two or three years and perhaps feeling his own time was drawing to a close, Motlow decided to honor his uncle with the commission of a life-size statue, complete with frock coat and planter's hat. The statue was made of Italian marble and weighed over three-quarters of a ton, and Motlow had it placed before the mouth of Cave Spring in 1941. That statue is now on display in the lobby of the distillery's visitor center, after being replaced at Cave Spring by a bronze statue of Mr. Jack.

That same year, Motlow suffered a stroke that paralyzed much of his right side. From that point forward, Motlow oversaw his business interests, distillery included, from either a wheelchair or bed. Although he didn't hand his business over to his heirs premortem, as Daniel had, it is fair to say that he leaned much more heavily on his four boys and his brother Jess during the war years than he had before.

Lemuel Motlow died of a cerebral hemorrhage on September 1, 1947. Although undoubtedly a flawed man, and one who would certainly attract some renewed controversy were he paid more attention today, it is impossible to conceive of Jack Daniel's Tennessee Whiskey as we know it without him. Perhaps, as an abandoned brand, it would have been picked up by Lewis Rosenstiel and, in keeping with that man's business practices, moved to Kentucky, Indiana, or Illinois and turned into cheap rotgut. Maybe it would have been revived only in the twenty-first century by a present-day Motlow, in much the same way Nelson's Greenbrier of Nashville was brought back by that family's descendants. Or maybe, without Lem Motlow, the brand and its style of making whiskey would have fallen into obscurity and stayed there.

Whatever outcome, Jack Daniel's would likely not have been positioned to be what it is today—American whiskey's undisputed Goliath and a cultural icon—without Lem Motlow's tenacity in securing its modern foundation. One cannot have Jack Daniel's without both Jack and his nephew Lem.

Lem Motlow's
Lem Motlow
PRIVATE STOCK
Tennessee Sour Mash
WHISKEY
DISTILLED AND BOTTLED BY
JACK DANIEL DISTILLERY
TENNESSEE
1/2

"The company put Lem Motlow's Sour Mash Whiskey on the market. The brand continued on for decades as a younger, cheaper version of Old No. 7 before being discontinued in 1990."

# The Motlows in Today's Moore County

When Lem Motlow passed away, the Jack Daniel's Distillery was the crown jewel in what was essentially a baronial estate that he left to his sons. He was the wealthiest resident of Moore County and its largest landowner. Those days are now very much in the past, as the family most closely associated with ownership of Jack Daniel's nowadays is the Browns of Louisville rather than the Motlows of Lynchburg.

That is not to say the Motlows withered into obscurity. As a family, they are still the largest landowners in Moore County, mostly through the family-owned Cumberland Springs Land Company. A visitor to the Jack Daniel's Distillery under their own power (i.e., not on a tour bus) would need to be quite inattentive to miss the stamp the family has made on the region, outside of whiskey making.

Most obvious is Motlow State Community College. Opened in 1969, the original core campus is located about eight miles from the distillery. Through his influence in the state senate and his organization of a family donation of 187 acres to the college, Reagor Motlow managed to get the college located in Moore County and named for the family to boot. That proved to be a far-reaching accomplishment—the extended Motlow college has campuses in Fayetteville, McMinnville, Smyrna, and Sparta, Tennessee. So, the Motlow name is now associated with a student body of approximately 6,000 in a region with over 600,000 people.

Reagor Motlow's largesse left his mark on the county in other lasting ways as well. He donated the land for the Moore County Public Library. Typical of small-town libraries, it is closed on Thursdays and weekends, and the Motlow name isn't on the building. All the same, most visitors to Lynchburg have probably seen this legacy of the Motlows (though perhaps not realizing the connection) because it is just down the street from the distillery's overflow parking.

The Cumberland Springs Land Company and its 6,000 acres of forest is now run by Mary Alexandra Motlow Richman, the great-great-grandniece of Jack Daniel. Richman holds a forestry and natural resources degree, and one of her duties in overseeing the family holdings is to manage its white oaks and sugar maples, trees that (directly or indirectly) feed right back into making whiskey at Jack Daniel's. The company sold some of its land holdings to Silicon Ranch for a $100 million solar farm project in Moore County that, when completed, is slated to be the biggest solar power project in Tennessee, and the second-biggest industry in Moore County, after Jack Daniel's. It seems that at any time since the beginning of the twentieth century, if you need land to start an industry in Moore County, you talk to someone named Motlow.

Motlows also tend to pop up in many other Lynchburg area businesses. Richman's mother, Mary, owned a local antiques store and Lynchburg Outdoors, a motorcycle shop, at the time of her death in a motorcycle crash in 2012. Visitors who explore Moore County will also find a number country roads named for the family. The living family is only directly connected with the business of Old No. 7 today through one member who works at Brown-Forman as an executive, but their presence in the distillery's environs is enduring.

MOTLOW
STATE COMMUNITY COLLEGE

MOTLOW

BARNS RD

SPEED
LIMIT
7

LYNCHBURG
HARDWARE & GENERAL STORE
"ALL GOODS WORTH PRICE CHARGED"
51
AED

JACK DANIEL DIST.
LEM MOTLOW PROP., INC.
LYNCHBURG
TENN.

# The Motlow and the Browns

JACK DANIEL'S
No 7

## Shirtsleeves in Wartime

Lem Motlow had four sons: Reagor, Connor, Robert, and Dan Evans, plus a daughter, Mary. All the Motlow brothers graduated from Vanderbilt University, giving the company's next generation its first college-educated leadership. None of the four started their career in the whiskey business due to the decades-long interruption of statewide Prohibition—unless one counts a four-year-old Reagor traveling to St. Louis with his mother and granduncle for the 1904 World's Fair.

Reagor, the oldest, was commissioned as a 2nd Lieutenant in the US Army for the First World War before returning to college and graduating in 1919. In 1922, he went to work for a mill in Union City, Tennessee, some 220 miles from Lynchburg in the far northwest corner of the state. Prior to returning to Lynchburg and the family's distilling legacy, Reagor also worked as an engineer in the Civilian Conservation Corps in Crossville.

One of the nineteenth-century mottos at Jack Daniel's that carries to this day is "Every Day We'll Make It, We'll Make It The Best We Can." The "Best We Can" part implies they aren't hidebound. Although the distillery values its traditions and prizes authenticity, that does not make it averse to adopting new technology or employing new ideas. This next generation of Motlows embodied this openness to change, embracing new approaches and philosophies that symbolized the rebirth of the company. They were dubbed "The Shirtsleeve Brothers" because they were often seen in shirts and ties (unlike their father, who was notorious for his casual workman-like attire) while at the same time not afraid to roll those sleeves up and get their hands grimy.

Although Lem Motlow did not follow his uncle's example by transferring the distillery to his sons before passing (he, instead, chose to stubbornly remain in control until his last breath), he recognized the need to train his boys in the family business following its restoration. Reagor, as the eldest, led the pack and became executive vice president in 1938, and then president directly thereafter. Connor stood as vice president, while Robert served as treasurer and Dan Evans as sales manager. Their uncle, Jess Motlow, was Master Distiller. Yet by the time Jack Daniel's was up and running again, it scarcely mattered who was calling the shots in Lynchburg once the Japanese bombed Pearl Harbor in December 1941. Just four years after the distillery filled its first barrel following Prohibition and numerous local political battles, it was still very much in the Lem Motlow Sour Mash Whiskey business, as the war put reacquainting America with Jack Daniel's on hold. Reintroduced at the end of 1939, the company flagship evolved until the early 1940s, settling as a green-labeled version of No. 7 with an age statement of three years.

To most modern Americans, the scale, disruption, and intrusiveness of the Second World War mobilization is wholly alien. The sale of new cars, including cars already ordered, was halted on January 1, 1942, as the domestic automobile industry retooled to war production at the behest of the government. New cars wouldn't return to the market again until 1946. Like most of his peers, Reagor Motlow received notice from the War Production Board declaring, "Congratulations! You've been chosen to make industrial alcohol for the war effort!" Those businesses were allowed to make money from the orders, but they were orders none could refuse. That alcohol was used to make antifreeze, medicines, pesticides, smokeless gunpowder, and torpedo fuel, among many other products. A 16-inch gun on the battleship New Jersey used up to 60 gallons of alcohol with every shot in just the propellant powder, to say nothing of the explosives in the shell.

Jack Daniel's Distillery made no whiskey from 1942 to 1947, because in addition to the government commandeering of their production capacity for the war effort, there was a ban on whiskey making after 1942. Also, resources used in making whiskey—such as grain, oak, and fuel—were all rationed during the war. Even if the greedy and unpatriotic wanted to circumvent the ban (as they did during the Prohibition era), they would find collecting the necessary materials a severe difficulty. Similar conditions applied to the whiskey industries in Britain and Canada.

As for sales of their existing stock, Jack Daniel's suspended sales of Lem Motlow Sour Mash, then their youngest product, to preserve their stock for use in No. 7 3-Year-Old. That wartime version of Green Label continued to sell until the company ran out of whiskey in December 1945. Thus, Jack Daniel's had absolutely nothing to sell until they were able to resume production of actual whiskey and had something old enough to label as Lem Motlow Sour Mash again.

The ban on whiskey production was lifted in 1946, but supplies of quality corn remained scarce. Lem Motlow's last major business decision at Jack Daniel's was a choice not to proceed with production until the corn supply improved. The cookers and stills weren't fired up again until 1947. Americans were able to buy a new Chevy before the Motlows were able to find enough corn to make resuming production worthwhile.

However, the new generation of Motlows was not idle during the war years. Besides making industrial alcohol, Reagor Motlow shared his father's taste for politics, and in 1941 he petitioned the US Treasury to recognize their Tennessee Whiskey as distinct from bourbon. Reagor probably did not realize he had embarked on a campaign that his company would pursue long after his passing—and one they would not win until 2013. Reagor himself was not that successful. The Treasury of that era concurred that what they were doing was not rye or bourbon, but "rather is a distinctive product that may be labeled whiskey." This vague statement was not what Reagor sought, but as the Treasury also did not object to his labeling, he turned the federal ruling around and declared Jack Daniel's special because of its charcoal mellowing. As the only distillery operating in Tennessee at the time, he tied that Lincoln County Process to "Tennessee Whiskey," making it seem intrinsic and almost unique to the state. Pre-Prohibition, charcoal mellowing was a feature of whiskey making across America, but it is unclear if anyone other than Jack Daniel's was doing it in the run-up to 1941.

Reagor continued his pursuit of politics after the war, before Jack Daniel's started producing postwar whiskey. He ran for and won a seat in the Tennessee House of Representatives in 1946. He then ran for and won election to the State Senate in 1965, spending three decades in state politics. His 1978 obituary in *The Tennessean* bills his role as a "veteran state legislator" above his work at the Jack Daniel's Distillery. But being a state legislator is often a part-time job, and Jack Daniel's was his business. In many respects, that business was primed for explosive success.

## The Postwar Era

Much is made of the federal licenses issued to deal in medicinal whiskey during Prohibition; however, having one did not matter a whit to the long-term success of a whiskey brand. The biggest name in Kentucky bourbon today is Jim Beam, and they didn't have a license. Likewise, Jack Daniel's was chased out of its home state a decade before national Prohibition, and they overcame their especially prolonged difficulties to become America's best-selling whiskey for decades. What led to this paradoxical reversal of fortunes—from defunct to dominant industry leader—are four key factors that are just as relevant today as they were in the mid-twentieth century.

First was commitment to quality. Lem Motlow abandoned his uncle's quality-control measure of only making 99 bushels' worth of whiskey a day, and his sons would expand distillery output by up to 50 percent year on year after 1947. Yet their choice to stick with quality ingredients and the added expense of the Lincoln County Process were elements that won Jack Daniel's a strong, early following that included many prominent figures. That word-of-mouth counted for a lot. Among the earliest examples, William Faulkner—a two-time Pulitzer Prize–writer, Nobel laureate, and noted drinker—was known to have been very fond of Jack Daniel's. Washington, DC, political lore has Harry Truman entertaining fellow politicians, such as the estimable Sam Rayburn, with Jack in both his Senate and White House days. Truman is also said to have sent a bottle to Winston Churchill, a famed lush in his own right. These were luminaries who knew a good drink, and they liked Mr. Jack's whiskey.

Another part of Jack Daniel's appeal was its easy authenticity. Jack Daniel's was a whiskey made in the middle of nowhere using techniques that were rustic, but also a little exotic. Tall tales and "marketing truth" are facts of life in the whiskey business, then and now, but the folks in Lynchburg did not need to stray from their everyday reality to sell their whiskey. Although fables grew up around Jack Daniel himself, what was in the bottles and the process behind it did not need any of that, and an informed consumer will always cherish the authentic. This began to figure prominently in the company's marketing from the mid-1950s onward.

Third was the force that was floating all boats. Prohibition, the Depression, and the war were finally behind Americans. The good times were back, and for the first time in more than a generation most Americans had money to spend and booze to spend it on. Aged spirits were scarce in the 1940s, and taxes on liquor remained high, so distilled spirits were much more expensive at that time than they are today, relatively speaking. According to a 1946 *Chicago Tribune* ad, a bottle of Old Grand-dad was $6.25, which in today's money is $105. Yet people were willing to spend their money and had something to spend it on for the first time in decades.

Finally, part of the reason that whiskey was so expensive was the taxes, but the other part was scarcity. Not even the bourbon barons of Kentucky had much properly matured whiskey in inventory, but few whiskeys in America were as hard to get as Jack Daniel's. It was the Pappy Van Winkle or Blanton's of its day, and just as with those brands today, the fact that Jack Daniel's was a hard-to-get commodity only bolstered its reputation.

The company deliberately played on the scarcity angle. They not only continued to advertise aggressively even as demand outstripped supply year after year, but in the 1950s the shortage even figured into those ads. Jack Daniel's advertisements of the era sometimes bore the message "We'd rather ask for your patience than your forgiveness." In so doing, they also passively implanted the idea that they were a hotly sought after item without bragging about it.

These issues and more combined to propel Jack Daniel's to national esteem in the 1950s and '60s, but the actual event that started the ball rolling was a July 1951 *Fortune* magazine article. It described an obscure Tennessee distillery that was making whiskey for Hollywood luminaries like director John Huston (his classic *The African Queen*, starring Humphrey Bogart and Katharine

Hepburn, was released that year), the sultry actress Ava Gardner, newly famous comic Jackie Gleason (the *Honeymooners* wouldn't appear until 1955), and the crooner and actor Frank Sinatra.

Nowadays, it would be easy to dismiss the power positive word-of-mouth or a single glowing feature in a magazine can have. Yet the huge push this *Fortune* article gave to the brand's recognition is undeniable and routinely cited in publications ranging from *The Atlantic* to Jim Stengel's book *Grow: How Ideals Power Growth and Profit at the World's Greatest Companies.*

Moreover, there are some modern parallels. Pappy Van Winkle was once a relatively obscure, small brand based on sourced bourbon, valued only by cognoscenti and noteworthy to the public only because it had very high age statements at a time when American whiskey hardly ever did that. "Pappy mania" came into being in the early 2010s atop the growing wave of enthusiasm for bourbon, which was largely built upon word-of-mouth and those eye-catching age statements. As the entire Van Winkle line became hard to get except at exorbitant prices, Josh Ozersky became the first to point out in print that W. L. Weller 12 Year Old Bourbon was made with the same stuff as Pappy Van Winkle and dubbed it "Baby Pappy." That one article published in 2014 pumped oxygen into a burning obsession among certain bourbon enthusiasts, first with all things named Weller, and ultimately with all things made at Buffalo Trace Distillery. And all this is in recent times, when the influence of word-of-mouth and magazine articles matter less than they did in the 1950s.

How the repute of Jack Daniel's spread by word-of-mouth is very much on display in that spell of Hollywood name-dropping above. Jackie Gleason is supposedly the one who introduced Frank Sinatra to Jack Daniel's, and it was probably Sinatra who introduced it to Gardner. A lesser-known story is that it was actually Lauren Bacall who introduced Sinatra to the whiskey, but the point would still be the same. Sinatra got to know Jack Daniel's because somebody in show business told him about it and/or gave him a pour.

It was also around this time that the whiskey took on the look and title familiar to us today. Jack Daniel's Old No. 7 with the black label was introduced in July 1953.

Jack Daniel's has been associated with a plethora of celebrities over the years, but none more so than Sinatra, who would in turn become the company's key unpaid spokesman of the 1950s. As Master Distiller Jeff Arnett put it, "Frank Sinatra took Jack Daniel's from a local, small brand to being a household name." Sinatra was at the peak of his fame during the decade, and Jack Daniel's gained from being known as the preferred drink of "Ol' Blue Eyes." The company, in turn, instructed Angelo Lucchesi, "the Jack Daniel's Godfather" and their first salesman, to make sure Sinatra was always stocked with Old No. 7. Thus, Sinatra was one of the few customers in the country who could count on always having Jack Daniel's on hand. The result was Sinatra declaring before rapt concert audiences that Jack Daniel's was "the nectar of the gods."

Yet success often brings with it more challenges, and the mounting demand for Jack Daniel's whiskey brought with it pressure to produce ever more when the Motlows' efforts to expand production hit a wall. As previously noted, federal taxes on spirits were high in the 1950s, and those taxes were always paid before sale at the retail level. Until 1958, the maximum bonding period (the time under which whiskey could be aged before taxes were due) was just eight years. As Chris Fletcher explained to me back when he was the Assistant Master Distiller, the Motlows had millions of dollars—most of their capital—tied up in the barrels of whiskey already sitting in their rickhouses. The company couldn't expand without either borrowing or selling off at least a part of it to outside investors.

But company historian Nelson Eddy points to a different reason for why the Motlow brothers, enjoying great success only a few years after the company's postwar rebirth, would want to sell: none of the Motlow brothers had a male heir to look to for the next generation of leadership in Lynchburg, and none would be coming. The youngest, Dan Evans, was already 50 by 1956. Their sister, Mary, had a son, James, but that line of the family was never seriously considered. As Eddy explains it, the whiskey industry of the 1950s had an unsavory reputation, and he believes that in the culture of the 1950s South a distillery wasn't the sort of thing one handed over to or through a woman.

Also, Mary's family was off in Florida at the time, and it is unclear if they were even interested in becoming involved in the whiskey business.

So, the Motlow brothers went looking for a good deal on Jack Daniel's Distillery, one that would protect the family legacy. Placing the preservation of their heritage above maximizing profit was what ultimately led them to accepting the offer of Brown-Forman. At that time, Brown-Forman was a medium-sized liquor firm best known for making Old Forester and Early Times. Based in Louisville, Kentucky, they were a family-owned and -operated company rather than a publicly traded corporation run from New York or Montreal.

These were features that reassured the Motlows about the future of Jack Daniel's, that agreements would be kept, and they personally would not be elbowed aside. Motlows continued to be enmeshed in the company after Brown-Forman bought into it. Reagor did not retire as president until 1963 and served on Brown-Forman's board of directors after the acquisition. Dan Evans subsequently became president and chairman of Jack Daniel's in his own right and held those posts until 1967 and/or 1968 (the records are unclear on when Dan stepped down from each). Today there is a Motlow working as a marketing executive at Brown-Forman, and other descendants of the Daniel or Motlow lines have consistently worked at Jack Daniel's in modern times.

To understand what might have happened if the Motlows had simply taken the highest bid, sold the company, and washed their hands of it all, one needs to look no further than what was happening with Four Roses Bourbon at that same time. The last of the founding Jones family passed away in 1941 and their company, Frankfort Distilling Corporation, was bought by the Canadian liquor giant Seagram in 1943. Four Roses Bourbon was one of the best-selling bourbons in America in the 1940s, but in 1947 Seagram foreshadowed their ultimate plan for the brand by introducing a cheap blended whiskey under its label. Four Roses Bourbon was withdrawn from the American market altogether by the end of the 1950s, leaving just the cheap blend, and, over time, Four Roses became synonymous with rotgut-grade whiskey. The brand's story has a happy ending with its revival under the ownership of Kirin Brewing after 2002, but it serves as a lesson in what may have befallen Jack Daniel's under the wrong owner.

Not everyone was as satisfied with the sale of Jack Daniel's to Brown-Forman as the Motlows. Another interested party was Lewis Rosenstiel, who offended Lem Motlow when he ran roughshod over their trademark on Jack Daniel's Old No. 7 in the 1920s (see page 53). As detailed in Reid Mitenbuler's *Bourbon Empire*, Rosenstiel offered the Motlows more money for the company than Brown-Forman, but they spurned him, possibly because he embodied the potential looting of their legacy that the Motlows sought to avoid.

View to east from entrance road near Deioinized Water House.

Panorama to north from reservoir.

Charcoal production area.

View to Warehouse #1-C and Motlow Home from entrance road opposite Bottling House "A."

View to northwest from Memorial Park area.

# Lem Tolley

Having done his part in reestablishing the Jack Daniel's Distillery and on the eve of World War II, Jess Motlow handed the role of Master Distiller to Lemuel Tolley. The job of sole whiskey maker in not just the Lynchburg area but the whole of Tennessee fell to a man who was no stranger either to the Motlows or to the work. As first name suggests, Tolley was a cousin, and very much part of the Lincoln-cum-Moore County whiskey legacy.

Lillian Elizabeth Motlow was the sister of Lem and Jess, and she married John Lafayette Tolley, who was part of the family that had owned the largest distilling business in the Lynchburg area when Jack Daniel was partners with Dan Call. Lemuel Lee Tolley, known to most as Lem, was born in 1898. Some folks called him "Big Hyde" because Lem was a tall, tough-looking fellow with a serious manner. John Tolley had also worked at the Jack Daniel's Distillery, so when Lem became Master Distiller in 1941, he was not just continuing the Tolley family's legacy in the whiskey trade, but also helping to foster the multigenerational workforce that so characterizes Jack Daniel's.

When Lem Tolley married, he moved into the Tolley family main house with what would become his new family, and his mother and youngest brother moved into an older house at 1328 Main Street. The latter building has been the Lynchburg Valley Inn since 2017. Located about a mile from the distillery, it is one of two places visitors can stay in Lynchburg that has a tie to the Jack Daniel's story.

Lem Tolley's tenure as Master Distiller was pivotal. He oversaw the switch to making industrial alcohol during the Second World War, and then the shift back to making whiskey afterward. Then, as the Jack Daniel's brand grew rapidly in the postwar years, Tolley was the man overseeing the massive expansion in production while doggedly maintaining the quality of the product. He was also working the valves at the distillery before, during, and after Brown-Forman bought into the company. Although this was an era when Jack Daniel's had only three products—Old No. 7 in the black label, Jack Daniel's Green Label, and, youngest of all, Lem Motlow Sour Mash Whiskey—Tolley certainly faced major challenges during his tenure. He was a pillar of stability during a time of transition and unrelenting sales pressure.

Tolley's reputation as a stern figure was buttressed by his work ethic. He worked six days a week and not infrequently on Sundays, as well. Sometimes he was even seen tending to business on Christmas Day, and he was not known for taking vacations.

Lem Tolley's son did *not* become one of the multigenerational employees of the distillery. Instead, John Compton Tolley went to Hollywood in 1943. Acting under the name John Compton, he enjoyed moderate success in the entertainment industry, appearing in supporting roles in films in the late 1940s and starring roles in television programming in the 1950s.

Tolley retired from Jack Daniel's in 1964 and passed away in Lynchburg in 1980.

The founder and head of liquor giant Schenley Industries, Rosenstiel handled in liquor brands as though they were little more than playing cards. He was reputed to have underworld connections and was close friends of the infamous shyster Roy Cohn. His fourth wife, Susan, spent decades claiming that in 1958 she saw Rosenstiel, Cohn, and FBI Director J. Edgar Hoover in an orgy with a couple of young blond men. That tale has been disproved, but it is indicative of the kind of bitter enmity Rosenstiel evoked. Even today he is known as "The Bad Boy of Bourbon." Rosenstiel was the type who would take the refusal of his offer as a snub, and a company being sold to a smaller competitor compounded the insult.

One of those many playing card brands in Rosenstiel's hand was Cascade Whiskey, which before Tennessee's 1909 statewide Prohibition had been made in Cascade Hollow, near Tullahoma, about 15 miles from Lynchburg. By the 1950s, the many twists the liquor business had experienced left the distillery abandoned and transformed the associated brand into George Dickel's Cascade Bourbon, made in Frankfort, Kentucky, at the OFC Distillery (lately known as Buffalo Trace). George Dickel the person was a Nashville area businessman in the late nineteenth century, who at one point owned a majority stake in the Cascade Hollow Distillery. Through that same deal, Dickel secured the exclusive rights to bottle and sell Cascade Whiskey.

After Bedford County legalized distilling, Schenley Industries built a new distillery in Cascade Hollow in 1958. Because of Rosenstiel's reputation, this is often portrayed as retaliation against the Motlows and Brown-Forman, but whiskey historian Drew Hannush points out that newly passed Kentucky whiskey taxes may have had just as much to do with it. The idea was to revive Cascade Whiskey using George Dickel's original records of the production process. However, Cascade Bourbon had been marketed as a cheap brand and had a reputation markedly inferior to that of Jack Daniel's. Instead of working to rehabilitate Cascade Whiskey, Schenley decided to name the new whiskey George Dickel. The first cases were shipped in 1964, too late to really take a chunk out of the continuing, rapid growth Jack Daniel's would enjoy.

The days of George Dickel serving as an instrument of revenge against Jack Daniel's are gone, and Rosenstiel's machinations may have even helped. Dickel whisky (the company drops the *e* for its products) was also made using the Lincoln County Process, and Daniel's and Dickel were the only two whiskeys made in Tennessee until the 1990s. That helped consolidate the identity of Tennessee Whiskey around the Lincoln County Process, even as that method remained first and foremost associated with Jack Daniel's. Even so, signs of Rosensteil's intentions with Dickel remain. The two main expressions of George Dickel are still named No. 8 and No. 12, an obvious parallel to Old No. 7, although the most recent labeling downplays the numeration.

“The founder and head of liquor giant Schenley Industries, Rosenstiel handled in liquor brands as though they were little more than playing cards. He was reputed to have underworld connections and was close friends of the infamous shyster Roy Cohn. His fourth wife, Susan, spent decades claiming that in 1958 she saw Rosenstiel, Cohn, and FBI Director J. Edgar Hoover in an orgy with a couple of young blond men. That tale has been disproved, but it is indicative of the kind of bitter enmity Rosenstiel evoked. Even today he is known as 'The Bad Boy of Bourbon.' Rosenstiel was the type who would take the refusal of his offer as a snub, and a company being sold to a smaller competitor compounded the insult."

George Dickel was not the only whiskey brand created to piggyback on the success of Jack Daniel's. The unsatisfied demand for Jack Daniel's left some proverbial empty shelf space, a vacuum that attracted imitators, the most famous of which is Ezra Brooks.

Frank Silverman established a sourced Kentucky bourbon brand designed to exploit the thirst for Jack Daniel's, and named it Ezra Brooks. Unlike George Dickel, which paralleled Jack Daniel's in some respects while also drawing on its own legitimate story, Ezra Brooks was a flagrant rip-off. As documented in the 1960 civil suit *Jack Daniel's Distillery, Inc. v. Hoffman Distilling Co.*, everything from the bottle shape to the color of the label to the text on that label was taken directly from the presentation of Jack Daniel's Old No. 7. Hoffman went as far as to make the entirely false claim in his advertising that Ezra Brooks was in short supply, copying Jack Daniel's advertising.

One difficulty Hoffman faced was in Jack Daniel's reliance on charcoal mellowing. There were no stocks of aged Kentucky bourbon lying around that had been filtered through hardwood charcoal prior to maturation in the barrel for him to buy, and starting from scratch would mean waiting for years to have a comparable product to Old No. 7 (which is why George Dickel did not first reach the market until 1964). Instead, Hoffman's company filtered already aged bourbon through charcoal after the barrels were dumped, prior to bottling. It's a key distinction and has a noticeably different outcome, but one that could be glossed over on the labels and in marketing.

The lawsuit went to trial, and despite the obvious poaching, the court found in favor of Hoffmann Distilling. It decided that the wholly separate name of the brand and its origination in Kentucky, not Tennessee, made Ezra Brooks distinctive enough from Jack Daniel's that Brooks could not be passed off as Daniel's.

The brand would continue to mislead the public about being a scarce whiskey in high demand well into the 1960s. Ezra Brooks would be traded between liquor companies many times, but as the years passed it would leave behind its roots as a Jack Daniel's knock-off, much as George Dickel outgrew its beginnings as an instrument of revenge. Now Ezra Brooks is owned by Luxco, also owners of Lux Row Distillery in Bardstown, Kentucky. To this day, Ezra Brooks is still made using charcoal filtration after barrel maturation.

Ezra Brooks wasn't the only Jack Daniel's imitator. Jim Beam introduced their own, Jim Beam's Choice. This green-labeled five-year-old version of Jim Beam was, like Ezra Brooks, charcoal filtered after maturation. At the time Beam's Choice was created, Jack Daniel's had just two expressions under Jack's own name: the black labeled Old No. 7 and the easier-drinking Jack

# Jess Gamble

Succeeding Lem Tolley was his longtime deputy Jess Gamble, who served as Master Distiller from 1964 to 1966. That two-year tenure was not a black mark against the man, but instead a mark of respect.

Gamble was born in Lincoln County, Tennessee, in 1901. Jack Daniel's Distillery was closed when he grew to adulthood, so that was not an obvious place of employment. He worked as a mechanic for the state highway department in Nashville for a time before he was hired by Reagor Motlow as an ordinary distillery hand in 1948. In the years that followed, Gamble forged a reputation as an industrious worker and dedicated employee. When it came time for Lem Tolley to retire, Frank Bobo had already been groomed as his replacement, but the decision was made to let Gamble take the top job for a short spell. As brand historian Nelson Eddy put it to me, Gamble was nearing retirement age himself and it was felt Gamble had earned the appointment as a reward for years of devoted service.

The odd thing about Gamble was that he was part of the region's embedded strain of teetotalers. Jess Gamble was a longtime distillery man and Master Distiller of Jack Daniel's, but he did not drink! Instead, Gamble did all of his evaluations with his nose. Although nosing is the first and primary tool for whiskey professionals engaged in sensory evaluations of the product, it is almost unheard of for someone to be active in the trade and not drink. The only example I'm aware of today is Steve Beal, a Keeper of the Quaich, who relies almost entirely on his nose nowadays for health reasons. Beal did not start his whiskey career that way. In Gamble's case, it is not known when he became a teetotaler, but he certainly hadn't had a drink in a couple of decades by the time he became Master Distiller, if he ever had. For him, not drinking was quite literally religion. Another noteworthy point about Jess Gamble is that he is the first Master Distiller of Jack Daniel's that was in no way related to either Daniel or the Motlows.

As planned, Frank Bobo succeeded Gamble in 1966. After retirement, Gamble lived quietly in Lynchburg. Although he kept a low profile, he did become a Squire in 1974. He passed away in 1988 and was laid to rest in Lynchburg's cemetery.

Daniel's Green Label. Jim Beam's Choice failed to attract major attention, surviving as a bourbon curiosity for decades, and was finally discontinued in the early 2010s.

Around the same time that the Motlows were negotiating with Brown-Forman to sell the company, Jack Daniel's struggles with meeting demand inspired the company to launch another innovation for the whiskey business: a fan club. The brainchild of Winston Smith, the company's first national sales manager, the Tennessee Squires Association was launched in February 1956. His idea was to respond to letters the company was receiving, asking for help in locating some Old No. 7, with a membership in the association that included an unrecorded square inch of distillery property. The idea was to make them notional co-owners of the Jack Daniel's enterprise. After that initial round of inductions, the only way to join the Squires was to be proposed by an existing member. Even in the midst of the contemporary Bourbon Boom, not every major American whiskey company has followed suit with a similar official fan program of their own.

## Soaring Amid Bust Times

If the Motlow brothers really did sell the company to Brown-Forman because they couldn't finance continued expansion, then the sale was eventually a success. According to Brown-Forman's official corporate history published in 1970, *Nothing Better in the Market*, they didn't finish the integration of Jack Daniel's until 1960. A few years later, they embarked upon a radical scheme to increase production without compromising output. Excepting the rickhouses and a few historic buildings—such as Mr. Jack's little white clapboard office next to Cave Spring—there was hardly a structure standing on the property that wasn't either demolished and replaced or else gutted for expansion and renovation.

Even after this expansion project was complete, the construction work stopped, and life settled down to just whiskey making at Cave Spring Hollow, the fruits of those investments wouldn't be seen for several more years. The increased output had to be stored away to build up stocks of whiskey, and then those stocks had to reach proper maturity before they could be bottled and make any dents in the thirst for Old No. 7. It's a story familiar to any bourbon enthusiast because similar situations unfolded at every major distillery in Kentucky during the 2010s—multimillion-dollar expansion projects followed by a wait of several years before those projects did anything to increase how much whiskey reached store shelves. Even though the expansion work took place in the 1960s, Jack Daniel's would remain on allocation well until the end of the 1970s.

For those who know just a little whiskey history, that Jack Daniel's would finally catch up with demand in the 1970s should make sense, because that was the decade of the Great Whiskey Bust. Sales of North American whiskeys (which includes Canadian whisky) peaked in 1970, but demand for whiskey generally went into sharp decline for the rest of the decade. The boomer generation generally rejected the drinks favored by their parents and switched to other options, wine and vodka in particular. American whiskeys acquired a down-market, blue-collar association that would take much effort to shed in the 1980s and 1990s.

Yet Jack Daniel's did not suffer in the bust. Actually, quite the opposite was true, with sales nearly tripling between 1973 and 1986. While their peers in Kentucky lost sales and chased customers with gimmicks like light whiskey, Jack Daniel's cemented its status as a cultural force representing mavericks and individualists, all while hanging on to a core identity derived from rural authenticity. In so doing, Old No. 7 went global. Mr. Jack's whiskey did this in much the same way that the Scotch whisky industry avoided the worst of the pain caused by that era's sales bust. Scotch had based its business squarely on exports going back to the late nineteenth century, and that diversification helped them weather the storm. Unlike most of their peers in America, Jack Daniel's continued to enjoy strong domestic sales while at the same time expanding rapidly into foreign markets. The Kentucky bourbon industry attempted the same but were not even close to as successful in their efforts. It's a testament to just how farsighted the Brown-Forman expansions of the 1960s were that they not only caught up with demand, but stayed caught up and found continued success.

Despite its reputation for traditionalism, Jack Daniel's Old No. 7 has not remained exactly the same through the late twentieth century. Production may have stayed essentially the same, but in 1987 the strength of a bottle of Jack Black Label was cut from 90 proof (45% ABV) to 86 proof (43% ABV). The expression was then cut further, down to 80 proof (40% ABV) in 2002. Maker's Mark made a similar move in 2013 and was met with general outrage by bourbon enthusiasts. By comparison, Brown-Forman said the strength cuts on Old No. 7 were to match the tastes of its modern consumers, and they were apparently correct about what those consumers wanted. Compared to the Maker's Mark reaction, the only aggrieved parties about the Jack Daniel's reductions seemed to write for *Modern Drunkard* magazine. In 2005, *Advertising Age* magazine declared hardly anyone had even noticed the cuts and pointed out that sales of the weaker whiskey had continued to rise despite (or because of) them. Croaking bloggers continue to gripe about these cuts to this day, but it seems most of those same complainants never actually drank Jack Daniel's anyway. If anything, in recent years Jack Daniel's began attracting the attention of whiskey cognoscenti while retaining its traditional fan base.

# Frank Bobo

Born in 1929, Frank Bobo was a Lynchburg native, but not one of the multigenerational employees that characterize the Jack Daniel's workforce. Instead, his parents owned the grocery store in the Lynchburg town square. Helping out at the Bobo's Market made him a fixture of small-town life there, which led to two stories.

The young Bobo's full name was Frank Thomas Bobo, and one of the locals who frequented Bobo's Market was one Frank Thomas. Mr. Thomas had big, bulging eyes, which led to his being dubbed "Frogeye." When Mr. Thomas and little Frank Bobo discovered they shared a name (give or take), the nickname was passed on to the boy. The old-timers in town continued to call Bobo by the name of "Frogeye" after he grew up, which was eventually shortened to just "Frog."

The other story coming from Bobo's boyhood at the family market concerns Reagor Motlow. As Lem Motlow's eldest son and heir apparent to the distillery that was scarcely a mile from the family store, Reagor was very much a local bigwig, and in playing the part he gave Bobo a nickel whenever he saw him. With a reward like that (at the time, five cents could buy a box of Cracker Jacks or any candy bar), one can imagine Bobo was eager to be seen by Mr. Motlow. The relationship ensured that Reagor knew Bobo from an early age.

Eventually, Frank Bobo went into the Army and served in Korea. He had been back for a few years, married, and was working in the family store when Motlow offered him a job at the distillery. He accepted and went to work there in January 1957. Bobo rose rapidly and was considered for the Master Distiller's job when Lem Tolley stepped down. Perhaps the fact that Bobo had only been with the company for several years played into the decision to give Jess Gamble his turn, but Bobo ultimately took charge of the still house in 1966.

This was a pivotal time for Jack Daniel's. Reagor had been retired for a few years by then. Although Dan Evans Motlow was president, the company's era as a Motlow family enterprise was definitely receding in the rearview mirror. Also, the whiskey continued to enjoy sharp demand and remained in allocation, and the Jess Gamble and early Bobo years were when Brown-Forman resolved to expand supply in earnest and at least try to catch up. The company tore down or gutted and rebuilt the existing plant, as Bobo and his team did their jobs throughout the process by walking around on temporary wood catwalks set up over and around the existing still-running equipment. Still House No. 1 went from two column stills to the five seen there today, and most of what one sees on a distillery tour in Lynchburg today dates to this time.

If one excludes Jack himself as owner-operator, and then discounts Jess Motlow's many years sitting idle thanks to Prohibition, Frank Bobo was the longest serving Master Distiller at Jack Daniel's, putting in 22 years. He ran the still house as Jack Daniel's grew from a national brand into a worldwide giant. Also, he finally caught up with demand and was able to see Old No. 7 go off allocated distribution in 1980.

Bobo's career also underscored how different the job of Master Distiller was, not just between the mid-to-late twentieth century and current times, but also between different major distilleries in Bobo's own day. In an interview for *Whiskey Lore*, current Daniel's Master Distiller Chris Fletcher (Bobo's grandson) spoke of how different his job is compared to what Bobo was doing. Contrary to the image of the Master Distiller poking his whiskey thief into the barrel, Bobo was concerned almost entirely with turning out new make whiskey. "In fact," Fletcher said, "once the whiskey's in the barrel, my grandfather never had anything to do with it."

That was quite different from developments in Kentucky in the 1980s. Trying to revive the bourbon industry after the Whiskey Bust of the 1970s, Elmer T. Lee would develop and introduce Blanton's in 1984, while Booker Noe and Jimmy Russell had taken to the road to evangelize their bourbons. Ambassadorship and product development are familiar Master Distiller tasks today, but Bobo was mainly found in the still house, working at mashing, fermenting, distilling, and charcoal mellowing. Through all 22 of his years at the helm, Bobo only ever made Old No. 7 Black Label, Green Label, and Lem Motlow Sour Mash. His legacy was growing output to the point that Jack Daniel's became one of the world's best-selling whiskeys, all while steadfast in maintaining technique and quality.

Frank Bobo retired from Jack Daniel's in 1989. He passed away in January 2020, and like so many others in the Jack Daniel's story, was buried in Lynchburg Cemetery.

# Jimmy Bedford

Following Bobo as the sixth Master Distiller at Jack Daniel's was Jimmy Bedford. He was born in 1940 in Franklin County, Tennessee. That county is separate and distinct from the town of Franklin, the latter being an upscale exurb of Nashville and in an entirely different part of the state. The Franklin County line is just due south of Tullahoma and only several miles west of Lynchburg, so Bedford was just a half step removed from being a local. That was close enough, in fact, that the family eventually moved and Bedford actually grew up on a cattle farm just outside Lynchburg. Bedford was already married by the time he graduated from Tennessee Tech University in 1962. By 1968, he was back in Lynchburg and working in the Jack Daniel's still house. After 20 years under the direction of Frank Bobo,

Bedford was named Bobo's successor in 1988. His tenure as Master Distiller was almost as long as his mentor's, as he stayed on the job until 2008. In total, Bedford worked at the distillery for 41 years, 20 of them as head distiller.

Bedford took over Bobo's role as chief of new make whiskey, overseeing the grain milling, mashing, fermentation, distillation, mellowing, and barrel filling end of the process. For a Brown-Forman profile, he once described his job in these terms: "The biggest constant in Lynchburg is Jack Daniel's Old No. 7, and it's my job to see that it never changes. If it does, I'm in trouble." He also used to quip that although he did quite a bit of tasting on the quality and consistency panel for Old No. 7, he would always spit and never swallow.

Yet as part of the changing times, he also took on some roles that Bobo did not, becoming the principal face of the brand. Jeff Arnett has said that when he knew Bedford, the Master Distiller spent up to half of the year on the road promoting Old No. 7 and loved the travel opportunities. It was an odd preference for a man who has been described as terse when not making a whiskey presentation, but it was a duty he shared with peers like Booker Noe and Jimmy Russell. Bedford's tenure also saw the introduction of the first two regular brand extensions the company had seen since its postwar era: Gentleman Jack in 1988 and Jack Daniel's Single Barrel in 1997.

For all his long service and renown, Bedford left Jack Daniel's under a cloud. He was accused of sexually harassing a female employee over the course of a five-day business trip in Texas in 2007. The accusations led to a $3.5 million lawsuit against Brown-Forman, which was settled out of court. Bedford was given the choice of retiring or being fired in 2008. Bedford was living at his farm, only a mile from the distillery, when he died of a heart attack not even a year later, aged 69.

EVER

WE M

WE'LL

THE BEST

DAY

AKE IT,

AKE IT

WE CAN

AWARDED THE HIGHEST
GOLD MEDALS
LONDON 1915
AND
BRITISH ANALYTICAL
CONTROL CERTIFICATE
LONDON 1958

# JD, Fans & Culture

Awarded The Highest
GOLD MEDALS
at
St. Louis Mo Exposition
1904
Liege Belgium
1905
Ghent Belgium
1913
Anglo American Exposition
London 1914
Certificate of the
Institute of Hygiene
London 1915
and
Star of Excellence
Brussels 1954
BOTTLED AT THE DISTILLERY

My earliest memory of Jack Daniel's dates to 1980. My family had acquired both VHS and Betamax players with a number of movies, among them *Animal House.* I was eight years old, but it didn't matter because I was a free-range Gen X kid—of course I watched the movie that was appropriately rated R. One of the iconic scenes in that film is the "They took the whole bar!" moment, when a bewildered and desperate Bluto (John Belushi) is thrown a bottle of JD as movers carry away all the suspended frat's liquor. He chugs it on the spot, wipes his mouth, and says, "Thanks."

Of course, it was cold tea in that familiar square bottle with its black label, which is often the case for whiskey when it appears as a TV or movie prop. The film was a comedy about college kids, very much marketed at the young-to-middle boomer crowd, and the first feature film produced by a humor magazine, *National Lampoon*, the 1970s equivalent to *The Onion*. That time in history was the lowest point of the Great Whiskey Bust of the 1970s, and yet there was John Belushi, at the end of his tenure as a founding cast member of *Saturday Night Live*, guzzling JD (not some trendy vodka) in his moment of distress. The scene is emblematic of how Jack Daniel's was still growing even as the rest of the whiskey industry sank and its place as an American cultural fixture. Insofar as I have been able to glean from books, magazines, and questions over the years, either no one remembers if there was product placement in that movie or there emphatically was not, so the choice of Old No. 7 was probably a personal touch from someone in the production.

Considering the place Jack Daniel's holds in the iconography of Americana, brand historian Nelson Eddy likes to say that Old No. 7 is the company's best seller, but the T-shirts are their second best. The look of Jack Daniel's is inescapable, not just in the United States, but around the world as well. So is the brand's distribution. Having been in bars that were often just scrap wood and corrugated tin sheeting with a bare light bulb strung from the roof, in places ranging from an Andean roadside to a Sumatran wildcat oil town, I can tell you that there are two bottles you will find most everywhere: Jack Daniel's and Johnnie Walker Red. But when you step outside, nobody is wearing "Keep On Walking" on their shirt.

The accumulation of so much cultural capital began with Frank Sinatra, who was a proto–rock star, inventing the role of the larger-than-life singer as he swanned about stage with his tumbler of Jack on the rocks in one hand and the microphone in the other. Following Frank Sinatra, Jack Daniel's became

“Considering the place Jack Daniel’s holds in the iconography of Americana, brand historian Nelson Eddy likes to say that Old No. 7 is the company’s best seller, but the T-shirts are their second best.”

JACK DANIEL'S
Old
NO.7
BRAND

indelibly tied to rock music. He went on introducing or sharing it with people for decades. Eddy once mentioned to me how he had seen a handwritten note from Bruce Springsteen from the 1970s about downing some Jack with Sinatra. From Frank through the 1970s, Jim Morrison, Jimmy Page, Tom Petty, and Mick Jagger were all known to be fond of Jack Daniel's, but Keith Richards and Motorhead's Lemmy Kilmister truly adored the smooth Tennessee Whiskey.

The theme of independent spirit often arises when discussing Jack Daniel's and rock music, but whether musicians were attracted to JD because it was identified with that spirit or if its association with rock music provided that identification is much harder to say. It is a connection the company continues to foster, as in 2024 they were involved in major music festivals like Boston Calling, Bonnaroo, and Lollapalooza, among many, many others. But Jack Daniel's has a cultural footprint reaching beyond just music. Creative folks of all stripes have embraced Mr. Jack's imagery and whiskey, and Old No. 7's reach is found in circles far beyond that, as well.

## Advertising the Down-Home Giant

For all the celebrity appreciation Jack Daniel's receives, at the heart of its resonance is a paradox—a giant corporate entity that was the world's most valuable spirits brand up to 2022, whose reputation is built on a small-town vibe and the traditional crafty practices so often depicted in its advertising. As Eddy maintained, "There is this tension between being a premium brand that strives to be accessible."

That tension should be palpable, but it isn't, and a large share of the credit goes to advertising. Jack Daniel's does, in most respects, have some bland mainstream advertising, indistinguishable from the aspirational advertising of their peers. The staple whiskey ad of the mid-to-late twentieth century said to the consumer "buy this, live the good life" in white-collar, upper-middle-class terms. Yet Jack Daniel's also launched some ad campaigns in the mid-century that were unique—that is, until they became an inspiration to JD's competitors.

That more distinctive approach started in the 1950s, when Jack Daniel's was so popular that a salesman could call on a bar or liquor store and they would take whatever could be delivered. Some of the advertising of that era was almost apologetic, but only almost. It struck that passively boastful note that the company would rather tell its customers to wait for a bottle than ask forgiveness for making a quicker, cheaper product.

A bit more Tennessee whiskey is coming your way.

MANY THANKS TO YOU AND YOUR CUSTOMERS for your patience during the shortage of Jack Daniel's Whiskey.

We appreciate your agreement with our refusal to hurry any part of the making and Charcoal Mellowing of our whiskey. And we're pleased to report that the modest addition we made to our small distillery now lets us produce a bit more Jack Daniel's without affecting its sippin' smoothness.

CHARCOAL MELLOWED
DROP
BY DROP

TENNESSEE WHISKEY • 90 PROOF BY CHOICE © 1960, Jack Daniel Distillery, Lem Motlow, Prop., Inc.
DISTILLED AND BOTTLED BY JACK DANIEL DISTILLERY • LYNCHBURG (POP. 384), TENN.

**KEY: THANKS—FYE '62—⅔ Page TRADE**

Come on down to Jack Daniel's someday and watch us make our smooth sippin' whiskey.

AGING A BATCH of Jack Daniel's calls for years of time and no small amount of footwork.

There are thousands of charred oak barrels in a ten-story warehouse. Full up, each barrel is too heavy to lift. So to get the whiskey properly maturing, our barrelmen need to kick them into place. If you ever tried to boot a 400 pound barrel, you'd know what these gentlemen are up against. But after a sip of properly aged Jack Daniel's, you'll be glad they're so fancy with their feet.

SMOOTH SIPPIN'
TENNESSEE WHISKEY

Tennessee Whiskey • 80-90 Proof • Distilled and Bottled by Jack Daniel Distillery
Lem Motlow, Proprietor, Route 1, Lynchburg (Pop. 361), Tennessee 37352

We hope you'll visit our distillery someday and meet some of the folks who make Jack Daniel's.

TOUGH OLD BIRDS like Herb Fanning here are why you'll continue to find Jack Daniel's so smooth.

Mr. Fanning has held every job in our Hollow. So he knows his whiskey inside out. And though he's long retired these days, we occasionally bring him back to check on things. You see, we know there's a certain rareness you've come to expect in Jack Daniel's. We can't ever risk changing that. And with prideful watchdogs like Herb on the scene, we don't think we ever will.

SMOOTH SIPPIN'
TENNESSEE WHISKEY

Tennessee Whiskey • 40-43% alcohol by volume (80-86 proof) • Distilled and Bottled by
Jack Daniel Distillery, Lem Motlow, Proprietor, Route 1, Lynchburg (Pop 361), Tennessee 37352

The more important campaign was launched in the 1950s and pushed strongly in the 1960s that saw Jack Daniel's play up its authenticity. Those ads were centered on pictures of either blue-collar men hand-rolling barrels or images of bucolic settings. They labeled the distillery grounds a "A Quiet Home for Ducks." Eddy believes calling attention to the town of Lynchburg—the multigenerational and very localized nature of the distillery workforce and their purposeful inefficiencies such as the Lincoln County Process—was very necessary. "The fact that they were doing it [that way] isn't enough. That would get buried," he said. Without calling attention to these things, Jack Daniel's would probably indeed be just another corporate goliath, akin to Coca-Cola, and who cares where Coca-Cola is made?

Jack Daniel's could afford to focus on some very uncool looking people and places to illustrate its methods and roots in large part because it didn't need to worry about being trendy. "In the 1950s and the '60s, the Hollywood connection took care of that," said Eddy.

The success of the "Postcards from Lynchburg" campaign—what has become known as the longest running ad campaign in American history—proves just how muted the juxtaposition at the heart of Jack Daniel's is. Eric Emerson, a comic whose deadly put-downs made him a feared stage presence on Chicago's roast battle circuit, is a Jack Daniel's fan and thinks the company's image contrast makes it quintessentially American. "I had a professor who did military work," said Emerson. "He used to say, 'There's no place too remote, or too anti-American, to find Britney Spears and Coca-Cola.' Jack is big, and it's not big because it's bad." Having been to some places that professor was speaking of, I have seen that point with my own eyes.

Mahmut Anlar is a Turkish artist and architect as well as a Jack drinker, and he doesn't see big versus authentic as being at odds at all. He said, "It highlights a balance between heritage and modernity. The brand's commitment to its roots in Lynchburg [...] adds to its authenticity and appeal. Consumers appreciate the genuine craftsmanship behind a widely recognized product."

Cave Spring Hollow earned its place on the National Register of Historic Places in 1972. The Jim Beam Distillery is not so listed, although the Beam family home in Bullitt County is. Buffalo Trace Distillery didn't join the list until 2001. Maker's Mark, a peer of Jack Daniel's in the "doing purposefully inefficient things" sense, was appropriately listed in 1974.

The history and the advertising all come home to those who make the journey to Lynchburg, although some get lost on the way. Eddy has said that every year they get calls at the distillery visitor center asking how to find them, with the calls coming from Lynchburg, Virginia. The distillery is unusual in that it has offered organized tours to visitors since 1964. Visitors were welcomed unofficially before that. For most whiskey distilleries around the world, tours are a twenty-first century phenomenon. Very few were offering them in the Lyndon B. Johnson administration. "I love talking with people that have visited there," says whiskey expert Robin Robinson. "The overwhelming comment they have is that 'It's in a dry county.' This paradox baffles and amuses everyone."

"I think that 'what you see is what you get, no apologies needed or given' attitude is a big part of the brand's everyman appeal, and the distillery and town of Lynchburg personify that," says Tom Wilmes, who writes about whiskey for *Garden & Gun* magazine. "On a recent trip to Lynchburg, some friends and I daydreamed about moving there and began looking up home prices." But not everyone who drinks Jack can or ever will make the journey to the western edge of Tennessee's Highland Rim, and that is what all the postcard picture ads were for.

# Yes, You Can Get a Drink in Lynchburg Nowadays. Kind Of.

One of the classic oddities about Jack Daniel's is how the whiskey is made in a dry county. Recall that following the repeal of national Prohibition in 1933, Lem Motlow had to overcome political obstacles at both the state and county level to reopen the Jack Daniel's Distillery. Despite Tennessee being the nineteenth of 38 states to ratify the Twenty-First Amendment (so people in the Volunteer State were hardly dragging their feet about ending the liquor ban, let alone stood opposed to it), the state government would wait until 1939 to complete the reversal of their own statewide ban. Even then, the legislature left the question of wet or dry to the individual counties, which gave rise to the legend: you can't buy or even drink Jack Daniel's in the place where it is made. Even Kentucky, with its many dry counties and distilleries, never had such a bizarre juxtaposition.

Of course, alcohol could be legally consumed in Moore County even before the 1940s. One just had to bring the booze with them. Preceding the modern Bourbon Boom, Brown-Forman sought to address the paradox of Jack Daniel's operating in a dry county. In 1995, the company persuaded locals (keeping in mind that many of those local voters are employed at the distillery) to approve a loophole allowing the distillery to sell "commemorative bottles" to visitors. It just so happens that those bottles were full of "free" whiskey. That was the beginning of what became the White Rabbit Bottle Shop, named for a former saloon owned by Mr. Jack himself.

That loophole gradually widened to allow for tastings at the distillery, and since America has this thing called equality before the law, the loosening of restrictions did not apply just to Jack Daniel's. Moore County is now what is called a "moist" county, a description that applies to most of the Volunteer State. Only 11 of 95 counties in the state are wet (i.e., permit the full, normal range of liquor sales by stores and restaurants).

In Lynchburg, it is possible to buy and sample alcoholic beverages in the place they are made. This has given rise to the Lynchburg Distillery, a classic example of a small legal moonshine company making flavored white whiskey—an aged whiskey that sounds like it should meet the standards for being Tennessee Whiskey despite not being labeled as such—as well as rum and vodka. Also located near the town square and right next door is Lynchburg Winery, which draws on the vineyards of a trio of local farms.

Beer and wine sales are legal at restaurants, although not all eateries in Lynchburg take advantage. Both of the barbecue joints in Lynchburg serve beer and there is even one spot called The Beer Garden. However, Mary Bobo's is (in)famous for *not* serving alcoholic beverages, in keeping with the spirit of Mrs. Mary Bobo herself.

Despite the exemptions, there aren't any regular liquor stores in town. Personally, I have repeatedly found myself wishing I could wash down a Mary Bobo's meal with a generous pour of Jack Daniel's because that menu calls loudly for a digestive. Still, the paradox of Jack Daniel's being made in a county where you can't buy a drink has largely, but not entirely, been resolved.

METRO
ORDINANCE
10-228
OPEN ALCOHOL
PROHIBITED
FINE 255.50

## Musicians, Artists, Comics, and Models

For many creative folks, their first encounter with Jack Daniel's was not as a cultural force, but as a gateway whiskey. In many of my interviews with performers and creators, Old No. 7 and Jameson were by far the two most frequently named introductory whiskeys. Such was the case with actress and model Carrie Stevens, who pointed to both attending college in Memphis and her lifelong passion for hard rock as steering her toward Jack Daniel's early on. "My favorite band was Van Halen, and they were always photographed with a bottle of Jack Daniels in hand," said Stevens. "So, naturally it was what I ordered as soon as I got my first fake ID."

She isn't alone in using Jack as a starter whiskey, only to fall in love with the brand. John Moran, an American glass sculptor living in Belgium, tells a similar story. "I first tried Jack Daniel's when I was probably 22 or 23. I was a big fan of Motörhead and I remember images of Lemmy having a bottle by his side at all times," he said. "At that time, Jack and Coke was my go-to."

Moran would later circle around to Jack Daniel's in his art in a series called *American Idols*. He described it as a "crazy installation" with hundreds of elements on American history and contemporary society. One idol was Andrew Johnson, the man who succeeded Abraham Lincoln as president after Lincoln's assassination. The artwork was called *Tennessee Tailor* (because Johnson was a tailor prior to becoming a politician and Tennessee Unionist). Moran heard Johnson was also a whiskey man, so he wove Jack Daniel's into his clothing.

Another artist, Marta Byrdziak, also recounted Jack Daniel's as her gateway whiskey. "I am from Poland, so for the most part growing up vodka was everywhere," she said. "When I was in my early 20s, I remember going to a party in Wrocław [...] and one of my friends was making Jack and Cokes. It was an early gateway into my love of different whiskeys."

Byrdziak would also return to Jack Daniel's in her work. "There is an idea that whiskey is not meant for women, at least in Polish society, so I began making my Box Glasses to represent a woman's love of whiskey," she said. "I love the fact that the number 7 symbolizes completeness and fullness, coming full circle in my mind to where my love for whiskey began."

Another early Jack Daniel's memory of mine is watching Robin Williams do stand-up in the mid-1980s, and part of his bit back then was to talk about the effects of drinking Jack Daniel's. It's not the most flattering of takes on what they do in Lynchburg (one part of the bit suggests the secret ingredient is urine), but Mr. Jack's whiskey is a common theme in comedy. A quick search of

Tennessee
WHISKEY

JACK DANIEL'S
OLD TIME
Old No.7
Tennessee
WHISKEY

JACK DANIEL'S
BOTTLED AT THE DISTILLERY
Kramer

YouTube will reveal plenty of material on the subject. Eddy has a story about a comedian who kept telling jokes about Jack Daniel's even though he wasn't a drinker himself. When asked about it, the comic said he would keep writing jokes about Jack Daniel's until people stopped talking about Jack Daniel's.

But some comics aren't just commenting on other people's taste for Old No. 7. They genuinely like it themselves, which is true for Eric Emerson. He has many memories relating to Jack Daniel's as a cultural fixture, but the one that sticks with him is watching Seasick Steve play the blues with a fifth of JD next to his chair. "Jack is reliable, affordable, and plentiful, and if it's there for you when you're down, you're going to remember it when you're up," said Emerson.

My favorite story about a creative person and Jack Daniel's pertains to William Faulkner, Nobel laureate and arguably the greatest writer of the American South. Faulkner was well-known for liking his drink, and whiskey was hardly his sole interest. But he was successful and middle-aged during the 1950s period when Jack Daniel's was, as previously described, the Pappy Van Winkle of its day. It is said that Faulkner loved his Jack Daniel's so much that he would serve another bourbon to his guests and keep his Jack to himself, as it was too dear to share.

## Food

Lynchburg whiskey is inextricably linked with food, and not just because of the store-bought sauces, chocolates, jerky, and other items that bear Jack Daniel's branding. The whiskey has long been associated with Southern cooking, especially barbecue. Going back to 1989, October has seen the Jack Daniel's World Championship Invitational Barbecue take over Lynchburg. The 2023 event drew 40,000 tourists for the weekend-long festival, which saw 85 teams compete for the BBQ crown. Mr. Jack's barbecue festival is one of the cooking style's premiere national events. Notably, Jack Daniel's does not show favoritism to Tennessee-style barbecue. The last time a Volunteer State competitor won was 2017.

Likewise, decades before any other distillery in the world had a house restaurant, Jack Daniel's had Miss Mary Bobo's, and that eatery should not be underrated. Every time I have sat down to a Mary Bobo's family-style dining table, there has been at least one person who made the trip for a weekday brunch from as far away as Nashville and Birmingham or else went out of their way (Lynchburg is out of everyone's way) on a business trip to patronize the establishment.

165

MISS MARY
BOBO'S
RESTAURANT
Call 931-759-7394
for reservations
www.missmarybobos.com

# Miss Mary Bobo's Boarding House

If anything else in Lynchburg is indelibly tied to the Jack Daniel's visitor experience, it is dining at Miss Mary Bobo's Boarding House. For an iconic brand with a global cultural presence, Mary Bobo's is arguably the most tangible connection to the down-home, rural, traditional facet of Jack Daniel's Tennessee Whiskey heritage.

Located just a few minutes' walk from the Lynchburg town square, the white Greek Revival house was erected in 1867, predating Jack Daniel establishing his whiskey business outside Cave Spring by almost 20 years. Built for Dr. E. Y. Salmon, a local physician and Civil War veteran, the house was one of the largest buildings in the area for some time, and during the years that Salmon served as county clerk his house doubled as the Moore County Courthouse. In addition to that, Salmon also operated a hostelry business from his home, calling it the Grand Central Hotel.

When Salmon retired in 1908, he sold the house to Mary Bobo. Before and after the Grand Central Hotel becoming Miss Mary Bobo's Boarding House, Jack Daniel would often sit down there for lunch. As the principal hostelry and eatery in town, Bobo's figured into the Jack Daniel's story in other ways. Lem Motlow's brother Tom, president of the local Farmer's Bank, rented a room in the house for many years. Her establishment earned a regional reputation for its delicious Southern fare, attracting the attention of any luminaries who passed through the area, including Eleanor Roosevelt in 1940.

Although Bobo was married, running the boarding house was very much her own business, not her husband's. She was a female entrepreneur, a rarity in early twentieth-century America—never mind in rural Tennessee. In keeping with the teetotaling spirit of Moore County and thereabouts, Mary Bobo never served liquor at her establishment, despite a good chunk of her post-Prohibition era business depending on the comings and goings at the distillery. To this day, alcohol is not served at Mary Bobo's dining tables.

Mary Bobo's ceased to be a boarding house in the mid-1970s. Bobo remained the owner-operator of the restaurant until her death in 1983, aged 101. Shortly after her death, Jack Daniel's Distillery bought the house and restaurant. The reopened Miss Mary Bobo's was managed by Lynne Tolley, the great-grandniece of Jack Daniel and member of Moore County's historic Tolley clan. She ran the restaurant until 2014 and is still listed as a master taster and brand ambassador for Jack Daniel's. Tolley is also the resident culinary author for Jack Daniel's, having authored or coauthored four Mary Bobo's– or Jack Daniel's–themed cookbooks. After Tolley stepped down, proprietorship of Mary Bobo's was given to

Debbie Baxter, who is there today. Baxter began her career in food service in 1978 under Mary Bobo's own tutelage.

Miss Mary Bobo's serves only lunch, reservations are encouraged (strongly encouraged on weekends), and the menu deals in Southern classics delivered in the family-dining style for a flat rate. The menu changes from day to day, but an example from one of my visits included fried chicken, stuffed peppers, green beans, fried okra, mashed potatoes, candied apples, and broccoli casserole. Cornbread and rolls are standards. Two desserts, also made daily (and usually pies), are offered. It's not quite all-you-can-eat, but pretty close to it, and on my first visit I learned to drop any plans for the rest of the afternoon. I have found that a Bobo's meal takes care of my appetite for the remainder of the day and sets me up very well for a nap to boot. There are nine dining rooms in total, and patrons are assigned seating. Visitors who arrive in large groups will likely be assigned a room all to themselves; singles or couples will find themselves sharing a table with others.

Dining at Mary Bobo's is not just a must-do part of the Jack Daniel's tourist experience, but a culinary tourism draw for the larger region. In my visits, I have found myself seated with folks who drove in from Nashville, Murfreesboro, Chattanooga, and Birmingham just to eat at the restaurant, and who had no intention of visiting the distillery. The food really is that good, and it's as authentic to that part of Tennessee as the Lincoln County Process.

Miss Mary
BOBO'S

As Southern cooking, barbecue, and whiskey have all risen in prominence together, cooking with whiskey has become more fashionable, and that includes cooking with Jack Daniel's. Christine Gallagher, an author and food columnist with Colorado's *The Daily Sentinel*, believes whiskey is more associated with Southern cooking because so much American whiskey is from the South. "However, that is changing as more and more consumers and more chefs around the world become more familiar with whiskeys," she says.

Gallagher began exploring cooking with Jack Daniel's by sipping on it while she baked, describing it as feeling "homey and comforting and like a warm hug." Two of her experiences in cooking with JD were naturals: a Jack Daniel's bread pudding and pralines. But she did have occasion to try something from a Jack Daniel's cookbook, Tennessee Wild Mushrooms Gratin. Her belief is that whiskey pairs well with umami foods, and said that "decadent recipe proved me right."

Yet when it comes to food, Jack Daniel's is sometimes compared to Kentucky bourbon. Despite being a cultural colossus and a longstanding fixture in barbecue, Lynchburg is still just one distillery and does not have quite the same footprint as the Commonwealth of Kentucky's entire sprawling industry. For example, although Nashville is a much larger and far trendier city than Louisville, it is a *music* town and not a *whiskey* town, and that matters in a narrow conversation about whiskey and food. During the 2010s in particular, it seemed like every sous-chef from New York or Los Angeles who wanted to open their own restaurant moved to Louisville, partnered with a bourbon brand, and set up shop in the Derby City. We even saw a little of that action in my home of Lexington.

"I don't think Tennessee Whiskey would ever surpass bourbon [in food], because the latter has many more high-profile cheerleaders," said Adrian Miller, a food historian and two-time winner of the James Beard Foundation Book Award.

Still, the operative question might not be so much how Jack Daniel's compares to Kentucky bourbon as a whole (which includes their own Brown-Forman stablemates of Old Forester and especially Woodford Reserve, which is deeply invested in food culture in its own right), but how it compares to, say, Jim Beam. And on that scale, Jack can still be described as the American whiskey with the strongest connection to food culture.

# Can Jack Daniel's Put Their Logo on Too Much Stuff?

Brown-Forman is understandably very protective of the value of the Jack Daniel's brand and is famously litigious in defending it. During my years writing about whiskey, they have threatened legal action or undertaken it against many whiskey companies, clothiers, and others with products that looked too much like their bottles, labeling, and logos. In 2023, they took *Jack Daniel's Properties, Inc. v. VIP Products LLC*—which was over a dog toy that looked like a Jack Daniel's bottle—all the way to the Supreme Court and won the case.

However, sometimes observers have found cause to ask in their opinion columns and blogs whether the party doing the most damage to the Jack Daniel's brand might be the company themselves. The JD logo has appeared on packaged barbecue pork and beef products, a variety of sauces, jerky, chocolate, toffee, coffee, cakes, spice and seasoning packs, and a truly dizzying array of clothing. Mind you, in an era when there are Jim Beam chicken wings on store shelves, it is probably unfair to post the question about Jack Daniel's alone of whether a brand can go too far and dilute itself. I suspect the reason JD is opined upon in this way is because they have had such a far-reaching food and merchandise presence for so much longer than any of their peers.

Insofar as the Jack Daniel's food products are concerned, opinions are mixed. Food writer Christine Gallagher disagrees with the take that Jack Daniel's has stretched itself too thin. "Having familiarity with a brand name can increase confidence. And if people didn't like the products, the market would show that." Yet food historian Adrian Miller feels that "it cheapens the brand identity. I once saw a mention of Jack Daniel's fried chicken. I thought to myself, 'Whuh?'"

My own view is that it depends on the product, not the idea as a whole. It is like when, as a boxing fan, I bought an Evander Holyfield cap. After I got it, I thought the cap was cheap garbage and the champ shouldn't have his name on it, not that Holyfield was cheapening his reputation by putting his name on so many things. In other words, I defended the "Real Deal" for the same reason I bought the cap in the first place. I lean more to Gallagher's position in this way about all the food products Jack Daniel's is stamped on. I have tried their barbecue sauces many times over the years, and some were quite good while others were flavored ketchup and not worthy of Mr. Jack's logo.

So, for the question "Is Jack Daniel's branding overextended?" the answer resides only in the mind that poses the question. "It would be like saying the same thing for Apple or Coke," said Robin Robinson, author of *The Complete Whiskey Course*. "These brands are embedded in the global front lobe because they are associated with so much more than what they're made of. They're a lifestyle, a cause, an affirmation, and an identity."

## The Two Circles of Fans

Bourbon fandom has always had a difficult relationship with Jack Daniel's. If you have ever seen someone red-faced and heatedly declaring that Jack Daniel's is absolutely not bourbon at a bar or a club gathering (and I have), that person is probably defending bourbon, not Jack Daniel's. As a born and bred Kentucky horse farmer's son, I have shared the general sentiment (albeit not the vehemence behind it) in the past.

My opinion began to change in my decade living abroad. In the Asia and even Europe of those years, if you wanted American whiskey, it was probably going to be Jack Daniel's. The realization that good things were taking place down in Lynchburg came much, much later to American whiskey enthusiasts.

"Prior to 2019 most whiskey enthusiasts outside their core fans weren't paying attention to JD," said Tom Wilmes of *Gun & Garden*. "For me, that changed with the first Coy Hill release."

That is a sentiment shared by Ed Escott, who leads Bourbon Obsessed, a club for bourbon influencers in the Bluegrass. "It was not long ago when mentioning Jack Daniel's brought sneers from bourbon enthusiasts," said Escott. "Then when Coy Hill came out, with its hazmat proofs, people really took notice and grabbed it up. Likewise, the older age stated versions also got people's interest."

If expressions like Coy Hill, Jack Daniel's 10 Year Old, and Heritage Barrel turned heads among the enthusiasts—who had previously employed snobbery toward Jack Daniel's—it raises the question: Did Jack Daniel's arrive late in producing the premium bottles that excite enthusiasts? Former Master Distiller Jeff Arnett has commented in the past that some folks around Lynchburg and in Louisville definitely had an attitude that Jack was its own thing. They didn't need to do what the rest of the industry was up to, and Arnett would know, since it was under his tenure that the company's practices began changing and a steady flow of new expressions came out of Jack Daniel's.

That late interest in expanding their line was well perceived on the outside. "They stuck with the 'if it ain't broke, don't fix it' approach even several years in the current Bourbon Boom and as big distillers started introducing products that looked and acted more craft," said Escott.

"While they did have some innovation," says Wilmes, "it didn't seem like JD was particularly interested in playing along on any kind of a scale. They didn't make a big effort to show the rest of the world what they were doing until maybe the Sinatra Select or first Heritage Barrel releases."

# Jack Was a Small Man, but He Left a Big Footprint

Although Jim Beam overtook Jack Daniel's as the top-selling brand in American whiskey in recent years, Beam operates as the biggest fish in the big pond that is Kentucky bourbon. Jack Daniel's, by contrast, is a big fish in a small pond. Sales of Daniel's ready-to-drink (RTD) cocktails—which are parsed out from the whiskey in industry reports—rank higher than sales of the next largest distiller in Tennessee, George Dickel. When Jim Beam announces a $400 million capital investment, it is undoubtedly big, but it also blends into news that Wild Turkey has a $161 million project and Heaven Hill is poised to open a brand-new $135 million distillery. When Jack Daniel's starts breaking ground in Tennessee, no other whiskey maker in the state is doing anything quite like it.

The data on just how large the economic footprint Jack Daniel's has in either its hometown of Lynchburg or in Tennessee as a whole is obscure, but the indicators are there. In Moore County, virtually every sport and civic organization enjoys sponsorship from Jack Daniel's. According to *BOSS* magazine, the company renovated the high school auditorium in recent years and is said to foot the bill for Head Start's rent and any improvements the local senior center might need. All that philanthropy plus being by far the single largest employer in Moore County is probably why a proposed 2011 barrel tax, similar to a now-repealed tax in Kentucky, was shot down by the county council in a 10–5 vote. As much as some folks want to squeeze the goose for more golden eggs, most are content with the eggs already laid.

The economic impact of Jack Daniel's extends beyond just their home in Moore County. Distribution employs truckers; production of sugar maple charcoal and barrels drives logging and milling across the state; even the public relations folks I dealt with while writing this book, who live in Nashville, are part of the knock-on effect of the distillery.

Perhaps most important of all is tourism. The Tennessee Whiskey Trail produced a study indicating that in 2022, the whiskey industry prompted just over $2 billion in spending at the distilleries themselves and in off-site establishments such as lodging, food, transportation, and other services. Over 300,000 of those whiskey tourists made the journey to Lynchburg in 2023, many of them traveling from Nashville on a day trip or as part of a tour group. That trip is 90 minutes and 75 miles from Nashville. Approximately the same number of people visit Buffalo Trace Distillery each year, but that distillery is much more conveniently located, sitting between Louisville and Lexington, Kentucky.

The Tennessee Distillers Guild is not really an equivalent to the Kentucky Distillers Association (KDA), and it doesn't sponsor handy economic reports stating in plain language that the whiskey industry has an X billion-dollar footprint in the state the way the KDA does. Nonetheless, a little reading between the lines tells us just how lucrative it is for the economy of Tennessee as a whole, not just Moore County, to host Jack Daniel's.

Those inside the company tend to share the view that Jack Daniel's has its own fandom separate from whiskey enthusiasm, although the whiskey enthusiasts are now moving in their direction. "Both those fandoms exist," said Master Distiller Chris Fletcher, who meets and talks with the two separate groups on a regular basis. "Different events will bring out different kinds of fans."

Here it is worth recalling that Fletcher was once an employee of Buffalo Trace, a bourbon distillery so feverishly beloved by a segment of bourbon fans that even their most mundane expressions are in danger of being bottle-hunted to extinction. Now back at home and working for Jack Daniel's, he is first to point out that "Enthusiasts loved Coy Hill, but every single drop of that would have gone into Old No. 7 if it hadn't gone to Coy Hill. And enthusiasts sometimes scoff at Old No. 7."

So, it might be late and it might be for the wrong reasons, but the whiskey enthusiasts are starting to come around and join the Jack Daniel's fans in their appreciation of Tennessee's leading whiskey. "There's some new movement there among the whiskey-wise," said whiskey expert Robin Robinson. "[The new expressions are] like tendrils from the nucleus that stimulate new audiences without taking away from the Steady Eddies that just drink Jack Black."

According to Wilmes, "Enthusiasts are more and more promiscuous these days and will buy something new, at least once, to try it." Of course, Old No. 7 can be a gateway that leads whiskey enthusiasts to a wide variety of whiskeys, but by and large folks such as the Squires and the hardcore Jack lovers don't wander. As Escott puts it, "I think the majority of JD drinkers are loyal to their brand and are not looking for something new."

The fans are passionate. Anyone who doubts that should Google "Jack Daniel's tattoos," but be prepared for some things that cannot be unseen. Eddy referred to that body art this way: "The power of a brand is expressed in how people brand themselves with it." Clothing, banners, and sometimes skin become a canvas where fans show their appreciation for the culture and lifestyle they believe Mr. Jack's stands for. It is a broad fandom that goes back decades, one quite unlike the sometimes-nerdy culture that defines whiskeydom.

## The Squires

Associations for fans of a whiskey brand are not as common as one might think. Maker's Mark has its Ambassadors and Four Roses the Mellow Moments Club, founded in 2001 and 2005 respectively. Both predate the Bourbon Boom, but they are still relatively recent creations of the twenty-first century. Most other

# Paying Respects to Mr. Jack

Although not part of any official tour in Lynchburg, no devoted fan of Jack Daniel's can call their experience complete without a visit to the Lynchburg cemetery. Most of the characters of the Jack Daniel's story have been laid to rest there. Some of those folks may have traveled widely as a result of their careers, but Lynchburg was and will always be home for them, now and in the afterlife.

Moreover, the cemetery is so close to the distillery that there is no legitimate excuse not to call upon it short of infirmity or ignorance, and I just removed ignorance. The graveyard is a mere two blocks west of the distillery's overflow parking lot, so only three from the visitor center's front door.

The main attraction is the headstone of Jack Daniel. The stone is flanked by a pair of white-enamel, wrought-iron garden chairs, making it easy to sit a spell with Mr. Jack. They say the first chairs were placed there for the benefit of local ladies, mourning the passage of the town's favorite bachelor. Even if it were true that the chairs have always been there, one wonders just how many lady mourners there were pining for Mr. Jack in the Moore County of a century ago, so I suspect that is another tall tale.

Every time I have stopped at the grave site, I have found at least one plastic shot glass there, so it is apparently quite common for visitors to show their reverence by imbibing a little of the modern Old No. 7, and just possibly sharing a little with the man himself. I believe the latter is much less common, however, because the grass has never shown any signs of dying. On my second visit, I found three shot glasses—two plastic and one glass—and a Glencairn, all left respectfully on the gravestone. My advice is to bring a flask; it feels and looks less like littering and reflects Mr. Jack's own style better.

Just a few steps away from Jack Daniel's grave is that of his successor, Lem Motlow, and many members of the Motlow family. Past Master Distillers Frank Bobo, Jess Gamble, Lem Tolley, and Jimmy Bedford were all buried at Lynchburg Cemetery. In the sense of the departed, it is possible to see the entire history of Jack Daniel's whiskey up to the twenty-first century in a short stroll of the grounds.

Football fans should also note that Lynchburg is the grave site for Johnny Majors. A prominent collegiate player in the 1950s, he would go on to forge an esteemed career as a coach at Iowa State, the University of Pittsburgh, and University of Tennessee before retiring in 1996.

Located across from Lynchburg Cemetery is Highview Cemetery, which is the resting place for a great many people bearing names familiar to the Nathan Green story: Green, Waggoner, and Eady. A memorial to Nathan Green has been erected there, although this is not actually Green's grave. His burial place remains unknown.

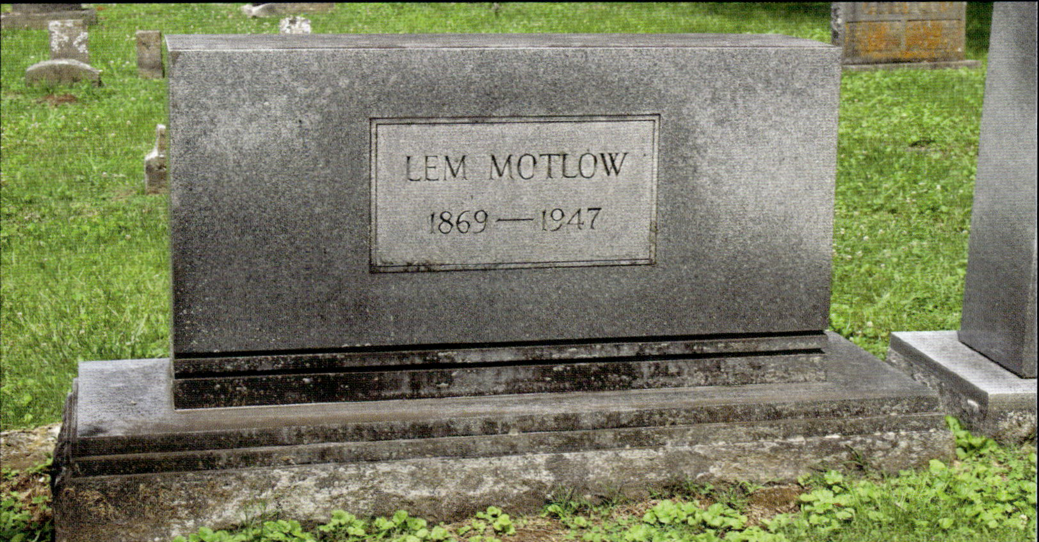

LEM MOTLOW
1869—1947

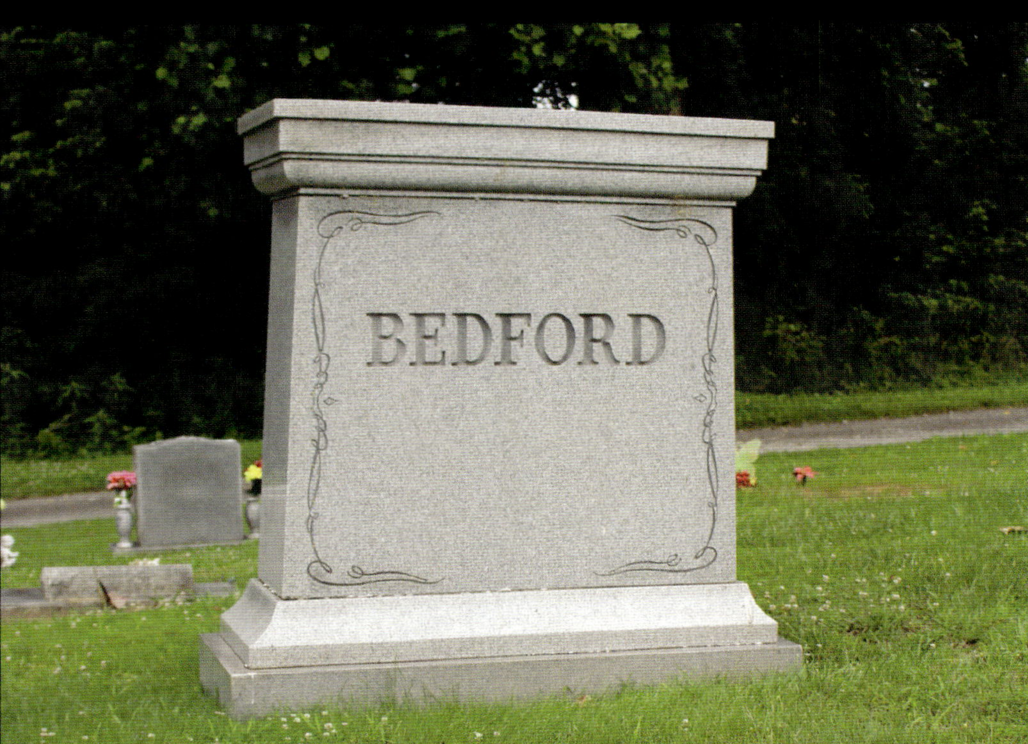

BEDFORD

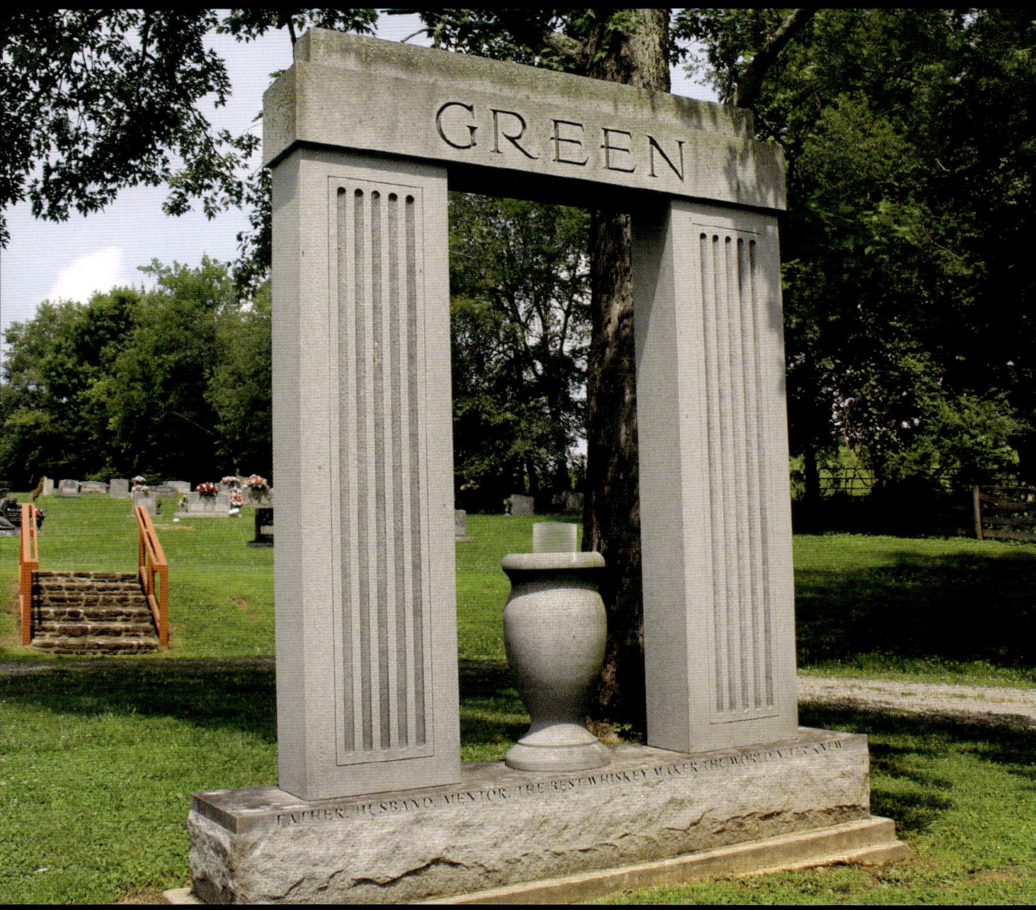

GREEN
FATHER. HUSBAND. MENTOR. THE BEST WHISKEY MAKER THE WORLD

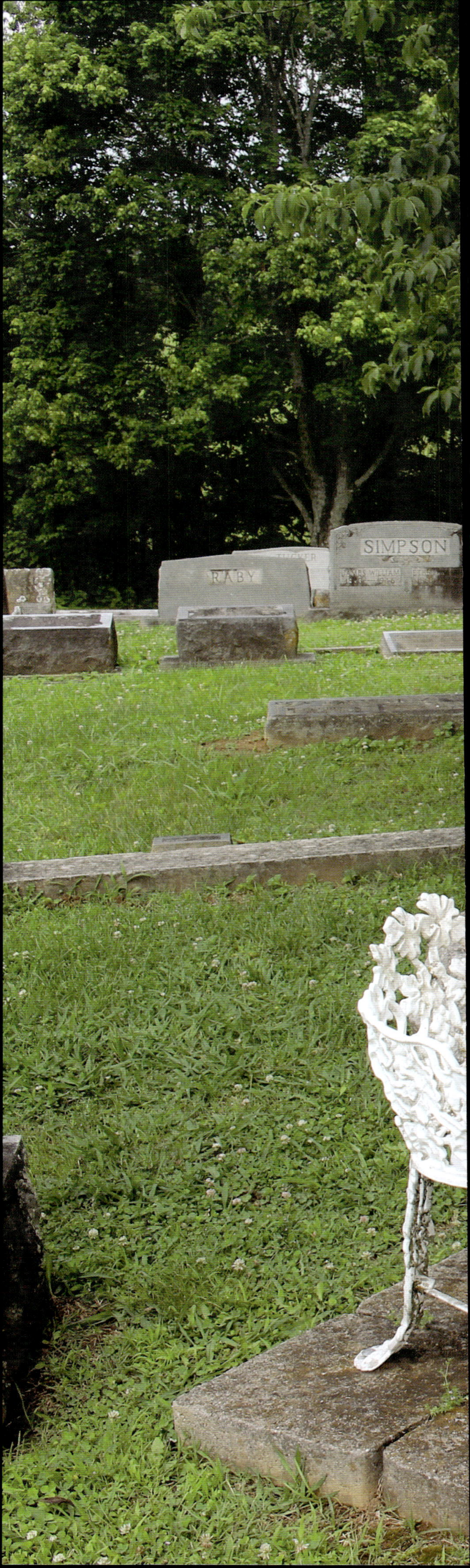
SIMPSON
RABY

JACK DANIEL
1850 — 1911
DANIEL

programs of this type are quite modest by comparison. The exception is the true grandaddy of whiskey-brand fan clubs, the Tennessee Squires.

The origin of the Tennessee Squires lay with the company's first national sales manager, Winston Smith. In the mid-1950s, Jack Daniel's was wrestling with being the Buffalo Trace of its day: people adored their whiskey, but they couldn't get any. In keeping with the times, when long-distance phone calls were expensive and email was still 40 years away, customers would write to Lynchburg and ask for advice on where they could find Old No. 7.

Smith was not able to help them with bottle hunting, but he decided to do something to reward their devotion. His plan was inspired by a gimmick he saw on a sales trip to Texas. An airport cigar kiosk was hawking the opportunity to buy a square inch of the Lone Star State for a dollar. Starting in February 1956, the folks who wrote the distillery would get a response back inducting them into the Tennessee Squires, granting them a deed to an unrecorded square inch of the distillery property. The idea was to make them honorary stakeholders ("Squires") in the enterprise. The association took off from there.

The first hurdle to membership in the Squires is nomination by an existing member. Current Squires are allowed to nominate three people each year. However, nomination is not a guaranteed invitation to membership. A prospective nominee must be of legal drinking age in their home country and should not be working in the alcohol industry at the time of nomination. In practice, that means no one employed in making, distributing, or selling booze. The Squires also have a Code of Ethics, and Jack Daniel's has been known to rescind the membership of convicted felons and folks caught selling their own Squires merchandise. Beyond that, those nominating a prospective Squire had better treat the nomination like a college application and write a good admission essay, detailing who the nominee is and their devotion to Jack Daniel's. The club is said to have a monthly induction quota, and there are some who have been nominated a few times before being admitted.

Squire membership has a handful of perks. Members have received a club calendar every year since 1994, themed around postcard-style pictures of Moore County life. The Tennessee Squires are also known to organize themselves into regional or local sub-clubs, offering members a social outlet to share their love of Jack Daniel's in places nowhere near Lynchburg. These groups hold their own events, tastings, and dinners and draw all manner of people tied only by Jack Daniel's. As Eddy puts it, "The banker thinks it's cool he's associating with the biker, and the biker thinks it's cool he's associating with the banker."

# Where to Stay: The Tolley House

By now the name "Tolley" has arisen in the Jack Daniel story more than a few times, and the Tolley House—a tangible part of that story—sits on the outskirts of Lynchburg, about a 20-minute walk from the distillery. This white Greek Revival house perched on a hill slope is as interwoven into the Tolley, Motlow, and Daniel families as those families are with each other.

Lillie Motlow was the eldest daughter of Felix Motlow and Nettie Daniel Motlow, making her Lem Motlow's younger sister and Jack Daniel's niece. She was courted by John L. Tolley, then a scion of the Lynchburg area's most prominent family, and the two were married in 1890. The location where the Tolley House sits today was but a part of the extensive Tolley family land holdings, which were so large that the area was dubbed "Tolley Town," a reference still used by some Lynchburg residents to this day.

Initially, the Tolley House was home to the extended Tolley family, but as that family grew the members of John and Lillie's generation moved out and into other houses erected on the sprawling Tolley Town properties, leaving just their family in residence there. Jim Conner Tolley and his wife moved into a house located across the road, and their daughter is Lynne Tolley, once the longtime manager of Mary Bobo's restaurant and still a key ambassador for Jack Daniel's.

Among John and Lillie's children was Lem Tolley, the third Master Distiller of Jack Daniel's. In his turn, Lem Tolley and his wife took over the Tolley House and raised their family there.

The ownership of the Tolley House and its ties to Jack Daniel's took an interesting turn in modern times, when it was bought by Fawn Weaver and her husband. They lived in the apartment above the property's Carriage House while Weaver researched her book on Nathan Green, *Love & Whiskey*. The couple also acquired the Dan Call Farm, which is just a short drive away, and started the whiskey company Uncle Nearest in Shelbyville. The Weavers no longer live there, but continue to own the property and now operate it as a bed-and-breakfast.

Along with the Lynchburg Inn, which is just a few minutes' walk farther down Main Street, the Tolley House offers distillery visitors an opportunity to stay the night in a place that is intimately attached to the people who are part of the Jack Daniel's story, right down to the modern era. In addition to Lynne Tolley growing up across the street and Weaver's own contribution to the Daniel story, a few of Lem Tolley's grandchildren live in the immediate vicinity of the Tolley House.

Within the Tolley House are three rooms themed for Lem Tolley (the Distiller's Suite), his wife, Ethel, and their son, the actor John Compton Tolley. Miss Ethel's Room retains her pink tile work in the bathroom, while the Compton Suite is decorated with posters from some of the Westerns and other films John appeared in. The Carriage House is a self-contained one-bedroom apartment. The kitchen access in either the main house or Carriage House apartment is especially helpful for dinner during an overnight stay in Lynchburg, since only a Subway and a Chinese buffet restaurant are open in town after 6 p.m. The house is comfortable and tastefully appointed while offering all the charms wished for as part of a country getaway. While many visitors to Lynchburg come from Nashville, those who choose to stay closer to the distillery for a night or two will be hard pressed to find accommodations as appropriate or agreeable as the Tolley House.

THE
TOLLEY HOUSE
— BED & BREAKFAST —
est. 1875
TolleyHouse.com

The best rewards of Squiredom come into play with a visit to the distillery. For starters, Squires have reserved parking places in the main lot, and that part of the lot is very conveniently located next to the Motlow House. That location isn't a coincidence, since one of the functions of the Motlow House is to serve as the de facto Squires clubhouse.

The original Motlow House was built in the 1870s and had fallen into a state of such disrepair after the mid-twentieth century that a true renovation was impracticable. As much of the original house was retained as possible, but it is more accurate to call it a replica or reconstruction than a restoration. The work was done for the 150th Jack Daniel's Anniversary and completed in 2005. The house is adorned with artifacts and memorabilia of the company and the Motlows, and inside is an exclusive club room for the Tennessee Squires, open only to those with proper identification.

Squires are also invited to special events at the distillery. For example, the launch of the Jack Daniel's 10 Year Old Tennessee Whiskey was celebrated by a special dinner and tasting just for members, hosted by Chris Fletcher and Lexie Phillips. The event came with a price tag, but tickets were sold exclusively to members of the Squires. The Squires also have their own tent and associated resources at the annual Jack Daniel's barbecue festival.

Stories about the Squires abound, and Nelson Eddy's favorite is one told to him by Jimmy Bedford. Apparently, a Squire told Bedford he never looked at his pour of Jack Daniel's before imbibing, because when he did it made him salivate too much, and that diluted the whiskey. I have never heard a bourbon fan or Scotch snob, no matter how die-hard, make such a claim. That guy truly adored his Jack.

My personal favorite Squires tale involves Boris Yeltsin, who was known to be too fond of Mr. Jack's whiskey long before he became Russian president. Back in 1989, when he was an opposition figure in the dying days of the Soviet Union, Yeltsin had been invited to the US. The Soviet newspaper *Pravda* slammed his drunkenness during the trip, and Jack Daniel's was mentioned in some of the press coverage. That was presumably his first experience with Jack Daniel's. The next incident with Yeltsin, DC, and Jack Daniel's came in 1995, when I was living there. The most raucous of the many versions I've heard was that Yeltsin and a few guys from his entourage downed a quart of Old No. 7 as guests at the Blair House one night, which led to Yeltsin staggering around on Pennsylvania Avenue, alone in his boxers, trying to hail a cab. Reportedly, he had to be rescued from himself by the Secret Service. Yet the conclusive proof that Yeltsin did indeed love his Jack Daniel's whiskey came after his death in 2007. Among his private papers was the deed to an unrecorded square inch of property in Lynchburg, Tennessee. Boris Yeltsin was a Squire.

"Yeltsin and a few guys from his entourage downed a quart of Old No. 7 as guests at the Blair House one night, which led to Yeltsin staggering around on Pennsylvania Avenue, alone in his boxers, trying to hail a cab. Reportedly, he had to be rescued from himself by the Secret Service."

JACK DANIEL'S
LYNCHBURG, TENNESSEE
JACK DANIEL'S
LYNCHBURG, TENNESSEE

JACK DA

STILL
Nº 1
61,714.3 wg

# How Jack Gets Made

# Chris Fletcher

When Jeff Arnett speaks about stepping away from Jack Daniel's in 2020 to pursue further ambitions, he says that the decision was shaped in part by the knowledge that a highly qualified replacement was already waiting in the wings: Chris Fletcher. Yet to whiskey enthusiasts, Fletcher was doing more than just taking over as the chief distiller and quality controller for a major American whiskey company. He was also advancing one of those things whiskey nerds adore: a distilling dynasty.

Fletcher was born in 1981 and raised in Moore County, but that is not the most pertinent reason he could be said to have grown up around the whiskey business. Fletcher's grandfather was Frank Bobo, Master Distiller at Jack Daniel's from 1966 to 1989. The Jack Daniel's story is very much one of intertwined families named Daniel, Motlow, and Tolley, and though Motlows and Tolleys continue to be involved in the company to this day, their legacy as the chief whiskey makers stopped in the 1960s. In the modern era of distillers named Noe, Russell, and Beam, it is Frank Bobo and Chris Fletcher who gave Jack Daniel's its own current dynasty of Master Distillers.

Jack Daniel's was a different place in the 1980s, and as the stories go, Fletcher spent some of his boyhood playing in the water flowing out of Cave Spring. After graduating from Moore County High, Fletcher chose to study for a degree in chemistry from Tennessee Tech University in Cookeville. After completing his second year of studies, he landed his first job at the distillery. Like almost all of the famous figures for whom making whiskey is a family trade, though, Fletcher's first Jack Daniel's job was hardly glamorous. He started out as a humble tour guide. Although the connection between the distillery and studying chemistry might seem obvious to us, it actually wasn't to Fletcher. He often refers to his summer as a tour guide as the "light bulb moment" when he saw how much his studies could be applied to the hometown industry.

After finishing at Tennessee Tech in 2003, Fletcher landed a job in the lab of Brown-Forman. He spent five years as a lab chemist and three more leading a production support group.

Fletcher then left the Brown-Forman lab in Louisville to move a few counties over, becoming the Lead Chemist at Buffalo Trace Distillery. He worked there from 2011 to 2013, and it was at Buffalo Trace that I and most other whiskey writers who knew of Fletcher earlier in his career met him. Often one finds that to advance with a particular company, one has to leave it, take a step forward elsewhere, and then return. Perhaps that is how it went for Fletcher, because after just 2½ years at Buffalo Trace, he was offered the Assistant Distiller's job back at Jack Daniel's.

As he describes it, Fletcher went home to Lynchburg as much to work for Jeff Arnett as to work for Jack Daniel's. The years spent serving as Arnett's right-hand man were busy ones. The years between 2014 and 2020 saw the introduction of the Single Barrel Rye and Straight Rye, Heritage Barrel, the Tennessee Tasters/Distillery Select series, and the original version of the Jack Daniel's Bottled in Bond. Fletcher always freely acknowledges his debt to Arnett and how much he learned during this time.

Fletcher has said Arnett's decision to leave Lynchburg and strike out on his own took him by surprise. Arnett stepped away in September 2020, and Fletcher's appointment to replace him became official the next month. Now with the formal title of Vice President, Master Distiller, and Director of Quality Control, Fletcher has been enmeshed in production at Jack Daniel's for a decade, and as time goes by the new products will increasingly bear his stamp.

Of course, Old No. 7 and its derivatives, such as Single Barrel, are very much part of the company's foundation. We can count on these to turn out more or less the same under any person's banner. Likewise, Tennessee Honey and the rye whiskey are Arnett's legacy. However, Fletcher's influence on the products coming out of Lynchburg did not begin when he took the top job. The 2023 launch of Jack Daniel's American Single Malt tells us that Fletcher must have been there during development. Some whiskeys are produced using the stock already in the warehouse, but anything requiring a new mash bill, entry proof, or specialized barrel stock isn't one of them, and the lead times for anything worked up from scratch can be measured in years. The Jack Daniel's take on single malt whiskey is just one example.

Fletcher has also shepherded the Jack Daniel's Bonded line into existence. That involved revamping what had been mainly a bonded version of Old No. 7 in one-liter bottles meant for airport duty-free shops into a generalized product, upgrading the principal rye expression from a straight to a bonded version, and developing the Tennessee Whiskey-rye-malt hybrid Triple Mash. The 10 and 12 year old whiskeys are also his creations, with more age-statement whiskeys to come.

Those who make Master Distiller at a major whiskey company tend to hold long tenures. There are examples where company culture creates an exception to that rule, but Jack Daniel's isn't one of them. Fletcher's grandfather Bobo and Jimmy Bedford held the role for two decades each. Arnett was there for a dozen years, and most outside observers thought he would retire in the position. Fletcher is still a relatively young man, only recently entering his middle-age years at the time of writing. All things considered, by the time Chris Fletcher leaves his post at Cave Spring Hollow, he will have made at least as deep a mark on what it means to be Jack Daniel's whiskey as any of his predecessors did.

## Water

Although the heart of whiskey making is always an industrial process—replete with chemistry, gauges, machinery, and boilers—the roots are always found in grain and water. Jack Daniel's relies on what is without a doubt the most famous distillery water source in the world, Cave Spring. Kentucky is celebrated for being essentially made out of limestone, but the Bluegrass is not the only location to enjoy limestone karst geology. It shares limestone-filtered springwater with many locations in its sister state of Tennessee.

Limestone filters traces of iron out of the water. That is especially important, because iron is otherwise commonplace in groundwater, and even tiny amounts of iron will foul the smell and taste of whiskey. With modern technology, some distilleries just use the public water supply and filter the unwanted iron out at their facility, but being able to skip this step is helpful.

But limestone does more than subtract certain minerals from the water. A given spring will have its own character and mineralization. The water used in making whiskey finds its way into the final product during certain key steps, such as mashing and cutting, so how that water tastes in and of itself is part of the identity of the liquor. To capture the idea, imagine using Perrier or San Pellegrino as the water source for making whiskey and how those might impact the taste.

The Cave Spring water is as much a part of the identity of Jack Daniel's as the sugar maple charcoal. Jack Daniel's uses an enormous amount of water: 800 gallons per minute. The company takes the security of their water supply earnestly, and own hundreds of acres of land for the purpose of protecting the spring. Former Master Distiller at Jack Daniel's Jeff Arnett has joked how much they all fretted over the outside chance of somehow damaging the flow of water to Cave Spring while blasting out the foundation for their second stillhouse (Jack Daniel's No. 2). Partner company Brown-Forman also recognizes their water supply is not infinite in abundance, so they don't rely on Cave Spring for every drop of water used at the distillery. Municipal water is used for purposes like cooling, and the company has implemented measures to recycle approximately 8 million gallons of water per year for use in their fire loop system.

# JACK DANIEL'S HOLLOW

Cave Spring, Looking Out—

Cave Opening 20 Feet Wide, 8 Feet High

Limestone Formation

Limestone Formation

Course of Water to Distillery

Pure Iron-free Water (Constant 56°)

Cave Spring—
Side View

Limestone Formation

Jack Daniel's Old Office

To Distillery

Waterfall

Dam

Jack Daniel set up his distillery in the Hollow because here's where he found the pure limestone water he needed to make his sippin' whiskey.

# Jac

# The

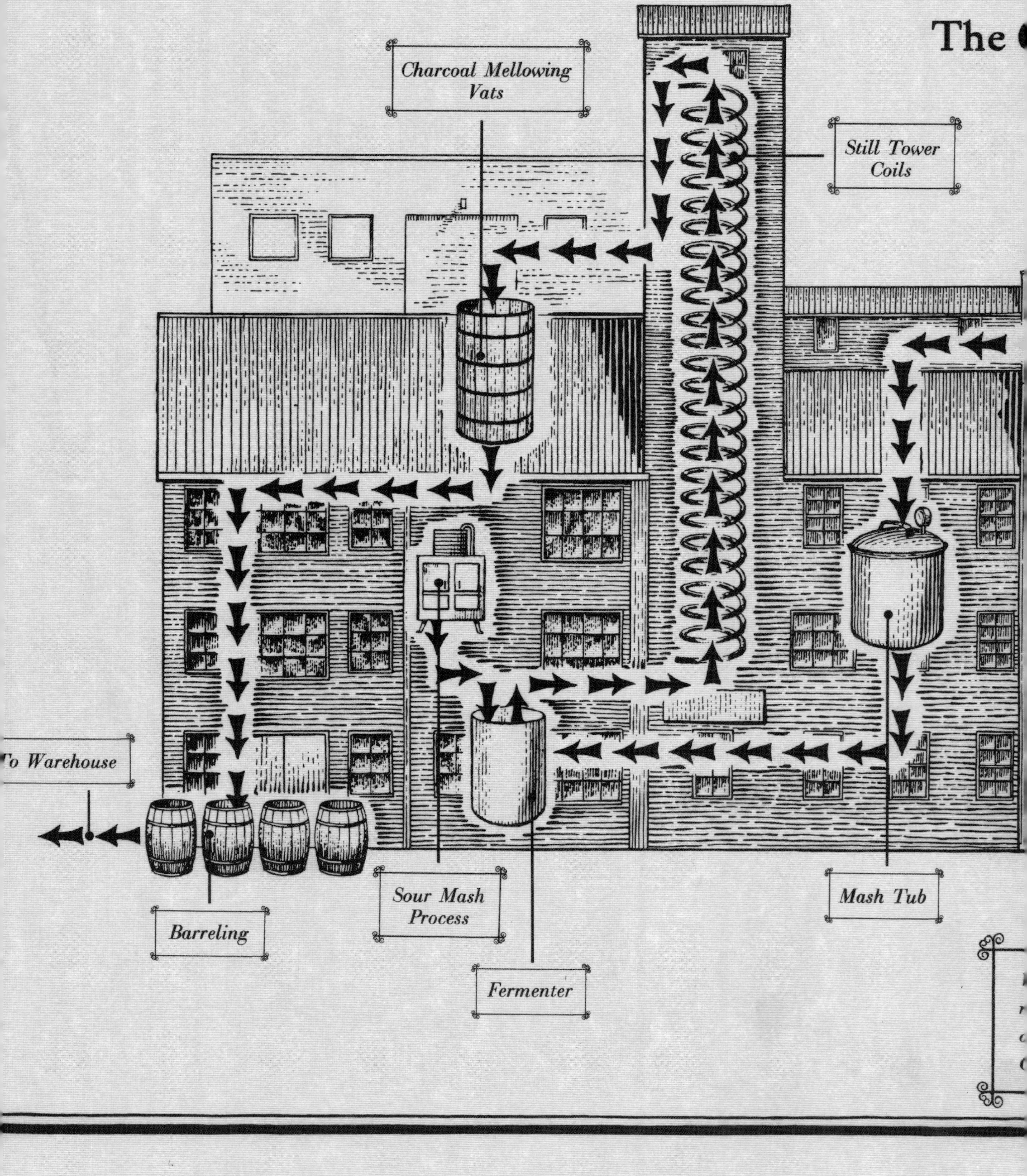

Charcoal Mellowing Vats

Still Tower Coils

To Warehouse

Barreling

Sour Mash Process

Fermenter

Mash Tub

# aniel's Distillery No. 1...Established 1866

# est Registered Distillery in the United States

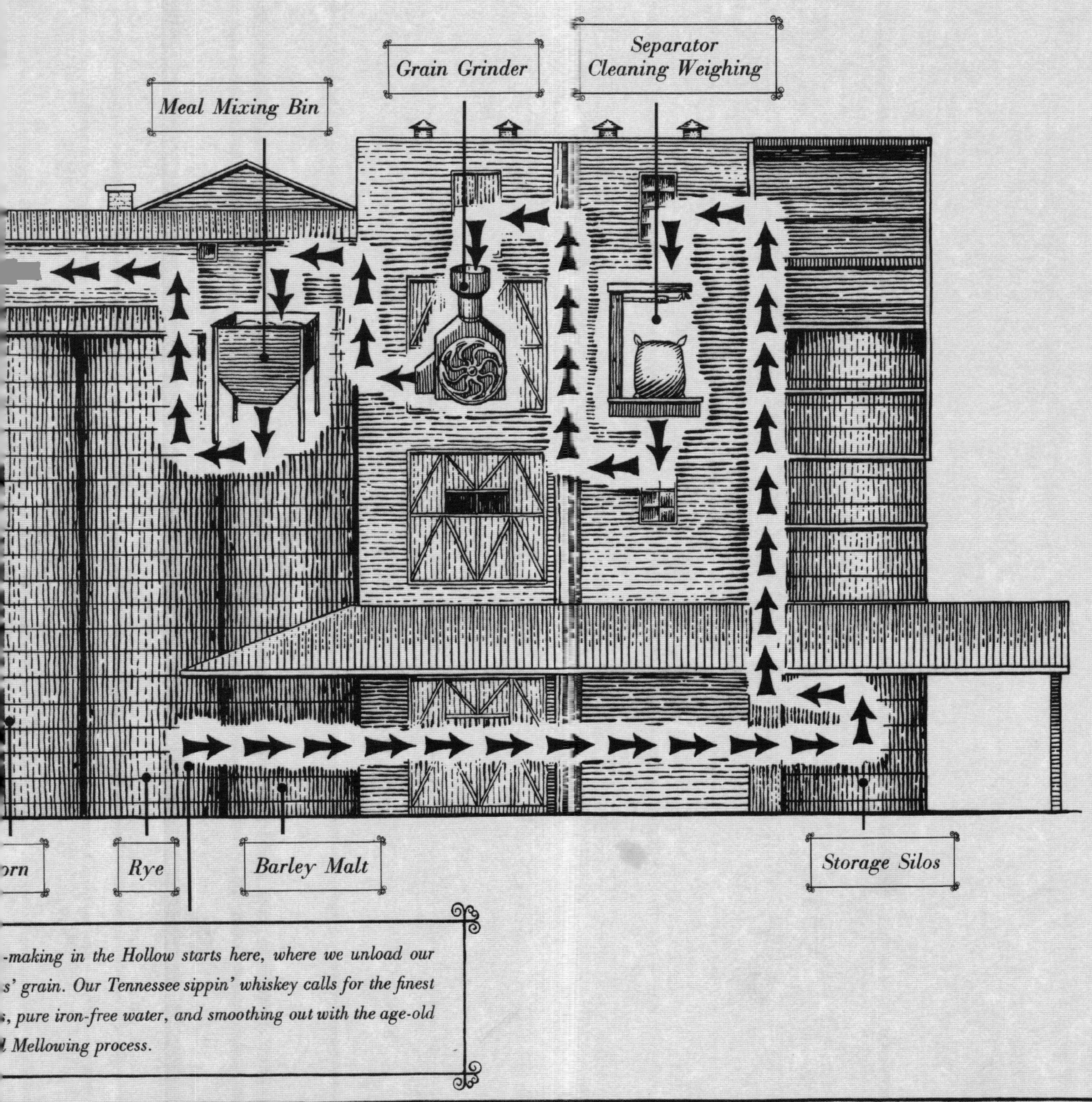

## Grain

As for grain, Jack Daniel's Old No. 7 emerged from the wider bourbon-making tradition, so like bourbon it is made with corn, rye, and malted barley. In the case of the core Tennessee Whiskey and the many other expressions derived from the same distillate (e.g., Single Barrel, Gentleman Jack, among others), it is more heavily reliant on corn than any bourbon made by a major distiller in America. The grain recipe (or mash bill) of Jack Daniel's Tennessee Whiskey is 80 percent corn, plus 8 percent rye and 12 percent malted barley. Whiskey enthusiasts refer to bourbons with an extra-large proportion of the middle flavoring grain—specifically to add flavor—as "high rye" or "high wheat." I've taken to referring to Jack Daniel's as "high corn" whiskey, because 80 percent corn is almost unheard of outside of actual corn whiskey.

At a time when small distillers often utilize specialized corn varietals in making bourbon, large distillers like Jack Daniel's draw on common field corn, known as yellow dent corn. American farms grow this type of corn in huge quantities to meet the needs of the industrial ethanol (i.e., alcohol for gasoline), plastics, and animal feed industries. Jack Daniel's says they consume 150 acres worth of corn per day of production. Not all acres are equally productive, of course, but if we assume those are average Tennessee acres, that translates into an estimated 765 tons of corn per day. While it may lack the flavorful aspects of heirloom white, Mexican blue, or Bloody Butcher red corn, dent corn is plentiful, and Jack Daniel's has been using it since at least the mid-twentieth century. Yellow dent corn is not just the only way to meet production targets, but is also part of the consistent identity of the whiskey. Furthermore, the distillery uses only yellow dent No. 1 corn, which is the higher-quality standard used by the US Department of Agriculture. Yellow dent No. 2 corn, the lesser type, is often described as the standard grain used by American whiskey makers. So, the corn Jack Daniel's uses may not be exotic or trendy, but it is above average.

Of the other two grains used in the Tennessee Whiskey recipe, rye and malted barley, the malted barley serves a vital practical role in the process of turning grain into alcohol. When barley is malted, it partially germinates and releases enzymes that help break the grain's starch down into sugar. With enough malted barley in the recipe, the enzymes convert most or all the grain starch in the mash into sugar. That conversion is crucial, because starch cannot be turned into alcohol directly.

In Lynchburg, they rely entirely on malted barley and its natural enzymes to turn grain starch into sugar, and no processed enzymes are added. The natural enzymes found in the barley produce complex sugars, primarily maltose; processed enzymes make simple glucose. Master Distiller Chris Fletcher

# A Tennessee Whiskey Mash Bill?

As already described, Jack Daniel's mash bill is four-fifths corn, an especially high proportion of that lead grain. This is so high that the only legal distinction separating Jack Daniel's and corn whiskey (which requires a minimum corn content of 80 percent) is aging in new oak barrels. Like traditional bourbon, Tennessee Whiskey must be aged in new oak, while corn whiskey is aged in used barrels. That one point of separation led me to wonder for years why Lem Motlow's Sour Mash was not converted to a corn whiskey at some point. The brand was, after all, always positioned as a younger, cheaper alternative to Old No. 7. The same cost-cutting logic lay behind the production of Early Times Kentucky Whiskey for decades, because that brand was a bourbon distillate matured in used barrels. Taking that same route with Lem Motlow Sour Mash would yield a corn whiskey.

That musing underscores one of the other signature characteristics of Tennessee Whiskey, high corn content. Although it's the Lincoln County Process that is inscribed into law, modern Tennessee Whiskey is strongly identified as high corn, and not just because of Jack Daniel's. Just a dozen miles away in Cascade Hollow, George Dickel is made using 84 percent corn. For decades, Jack Daniel's and George Dickel were the only whiskey distilleries in Tennessee. The pair was not joined by Prichard's Distillery until 1997, and it would be another 15 years after Prichard's opened before the first of the now dozens of other craft and medium-sized distillers would enter the Volunteer State scene.

All manner of mash bills were utilized in Tennessee prior to Prohibition. Nelson's Greenbrier, as just one example using a historically inspired recipe, is a wheated Tennessee Whiskey with a mash bill that would otherwise be entirely in keeping with regular bourbon. But for a long time, the only Tennessee Whiskeys on the market were both high corn, and even today Jack Daniel's and George Dickel account for almost all the Tennessee Whiskey sitting on bar and store shelves. The law requires Tennessee Whiskey to use the Lincoln County Process, so that is the main signature of the style. But on the taste buds of many, the sweet, high corn mash bill is the second signature.

Corn
CORN
Barley

BARLEY
Rye
RYE

explains it this way: "Malted barley is like a pair of scissors, slowly snipping away at the starch, while [processed enzymes] are like a shotgun blast." They believe the resulting sugars are better for fermentation.

Rye is used in a bourbon mash bill to add a spicy kick to the yellow corn sweetness. Old Forester, a Brown-Forman stablemate of Jack Daniel's, uses 18 percent rye. Jim Beam and Wild Turkey both use 13 percent rye. Lynchburg uses an exceptionally low 8 percent, but more rye would mean a spicier flavor, which is incompatible with the distinctive mellowness of Old No. 7. In the early 2010s, that one mash bill would have been the end of the story for Jack Daniel's, but nowadays they have a rye whiskey and an American single malt whiskey. The grain used for the single malt is easy enough to explain. Like its Scottish, Irish, and Japanese cousins, the mash bill is 100 percent malted barley. The Jack Daniel's rye is 70 percent rye, 18 percent corn, and 12 percent malted barley. For a brand known for its mellowness, choosing to go with 70 percent rye is paradoxical, since that proportion is better associated with bold Maryland-style rye whiskey. Nonetheless, it mirrors the very corn-forward mash bill of Old No. 7 by being rye-forward, and in that sense suits Jack Daniel's better than a sweeter Kentucky-style rye would at closer to 50 percent.

After the grain is delivered and de-stoned, the next step is milling, which takes place at one of two facilities at the distillery. The plant that tourists see dates back to at least the 1960s expansion project, if not earlier in parts, and is known colloquially as "JD 1." The stillhouse itself bears that language: Jack Daniel's Distillery No. 1. According to Jack Daniel's historian Nelson Eddy, "Most of what you see today is from the Frank Bobo era. The mid-2010s expansion project resulted in 'JD 2,' located over the hill and out of sight." People outside the company rarely ever see JD 2 in the flesh, but it is easy to see on the internet. Search the Jack Daniel's Distillery on Google Maps and look for the JD 2 facility to the northeast. The 10-million-gallon water holding tank and pipelines are conspicuous landmarks.

According to CST, who built the grain silos for JD 2, the new silos incorporate the mills right into the silo complex. That innovation is more efficient, as it saves on transporting grain to and from the mill, as well as on the construction of a separate mill building or annex. As a result, there is a separate complex of four silos each for corn, rye, and malted barley. Jeff Arnett described the arrangement as a "universal grain mill." JD 1 employs the traditional arrangement of keeping the mills separate from the silos. What results from these differences between JD 1 and JD 2 at the milling stage is that all rye and malt whiskey made in Lynchburg is made at JD 2; the larger original JD 1 is devoted solely to the corn-hungry Tennessee Whiskey. In 2021, JD 1 milled 30 tons of corn per hour.

# What Happens to the Leftovers?

Despite recycling up to 30 percent of a batch of fermented mash as setback for the sour mash process, going through 150 acres of corn plus a sizable amount of barley and rye per day means Jack Daniel's makes not just a lot of whiskey. The distillery also produces a staggering amount of waste, in the form of grainy slurry.

That slurry is called "stillage" in the whiskey industry, and the traditional answer to the problem of what to do with it goes all the way back to the days of the farmer-distiller: feed it to livestock. Although the starch has been largely depleted for fermentation, the protein and oils found in the cereals are still there. Stillage is also typically nine-tenths water, so to cattle and pigs in particular it is basically a farmyard version of a protein powder drink. As I was growing up on a horse farm in the Kentucky Bluegrass, watching surrounding cattle farmers feed bourbon distillery stillage to their livestock was a fixture when I was driving to and from the farm. In the decades before the twenty-first century Bourbon Boom, a big whiskey distiller like Jack Daniel's could simply sell their stillage disposal problem away. Local farmers would come fetch it in tankers and carry it off at the (current) bargain price of 50 cents per ton. According to *AG Proud*, some 200 farmers within a 20-mile radius of Jack Daniel's Distillery rely on its stillage to feed their animals. The Tennessee version calls for mixing hay into the stillage to add fiber.

But production on Lynchburg's current scale means that relying on local cattle to slurp down the stillage simply does not cut it anymore. In a 2022 interview for *The Lynchburg Times*, Jack Daniel's claimed to be dealing with 500,000 gallons of grainy wastewater per day. Part of the problem is storage, because even if the storage tanks were available for an interim period, the stuff spoils after two or three days during warm months. Being mostly water, the stillage is prone to freezing during the winter season. Jack Daniel's also operates what is called a dry house, where stillage is heated and partly dehydrated into dried distillers grains, which has a longer shelf life. They process approximately four-tenths of their stillage in this way. That helps with the shelf life and freezing problems, but the process is energy intensive.

With an eye on its sustainability (and perhaps earning more revenue for its stillage), Jack Daniel's is borrowing a page from the movie *Mad Max: Beyond Thunderdome* and turning the stillage it can't feed to cows into natural gas. Starting in January 2023, the company entered into a partnership with Michigan's 3 Rivers Energy Partners (who in turn partnered with Wisconsin's BIOFerm) to build an anaerobic digester at the distillery. This facility will turn the stillage into natural gas, with the leftover solids becoming low-carbon fertilizer. A BioFerm engineer told *The Cap Times* that the digester would reduce Jack Daniel's energy use by 30 percent by cutting back on its stillage drying, while producing enough natural gas for electricity to power 11,500 cars annually.

Although some local farmers weren't happy with the news that their cheap stillage was going to be diverted to natural gas, it needs to be remembered just how fast and by how much Jack Daniel's production has grown. Just several years ago, company marketing was saying they were using 95 acres of corn per day, so corn consumption has grown by roughly a third in that time. Reporting from *AG Daily* stated that the energy project was expected to consume roughly three-fifths of the daily stillage output, leaving an amount of "slop" for farmers comparable to what was available to them 15 or 20 years ago. While the energy project's scope could increase in the future, so could the stillage output from Jack Daniel's, as JD 2 was designed with multiple future expansions in mind. Although it is entirely conceivable that Jack Daniel's might lead the way in becoming a sustainable distillery energy producer—pivoting away from stillage feed altogether and making a lot of local cattle farmers very unhappy—reading between the lines suggests that for the middle term we should see the company's energy bills get a lot lighter as they mothball their dry house operation, leaving plenty of liquid slop for those hungry cows.

GRAIN MILL

After milling, water from Cave Spring is added to the individual rough flours, making those separate mashes of grain and water ready for cooking. Jack Daniel's is known for making a relatively thick mash, with less water than some other major American whiskey makers. But before the mash enters the cooker, the setback goes in, which is where the whiskey picks up its "sour mash" designation. The sour mash whiskey process was first codified by Dr. James Crow, a Scottish physician and chemist who immigrated to Kentucky and worked in the Kentucky bourbon industry from the 1830s to the 1850s. Coincidentally, the distillery Crow worked at for most of his career is now Woodford Reserve, owned by Brown-Forman.

Setback is the leftovers from a previous round of fermentation, after the liquid has been pumped away and sent for distillation. This setback was dubbed "sour" because of its acidity, which prevents bacterial contamination in a new batch of mash. The leftovers also contain some of the distiller's yeast, and having a little of the desired yeast present helps keep wild yeast (present everywhere in the air) out of the mash. This process allows for consistency from mash to mash. In Lynchburg, up to 30 percent of a new batch of mash will be setback.

In the larger bourbon industry, the terms *setback* and *backset* are often used interchangeably. What they mean might change depending on where they are used, and that difference is sometimes a fixture of a distillery's work culture. At Jack Daniel's, if one refers to the thin stillage going into the new mash, that is *setback*. They use the term *backset* in reference to setting a yeast tub from one pumping to a fermenter.

The corn mash goes into the cookers first, as it requires the longest cook time and the highest cooking temperature at approximately 212°F, the boiling point of water. After cooking, the corn mash is allowed to cool down to 170°F, the cooking point for the rye mash. The cooling and cooking process is repeated by bringing the temperature down to 148°F and adding the malted barley mash. The grains are mixed and cooked in this way because each has a different ideal temperature for making their starches soluble, which in turn optimizes the conversion of starch to sugar. All three grains are now cooked and mixed as a sugary grain slurry and allowed to cool down to 75°F, at which point it is ready for fermentation. At Jack Daniel's, the entire cooking process takes about two hours from first addition to pump out.

The distillery refers to its fermenters in terms of 40,000-gallon units because most of the 80 fermenters in operation are that size. However, JD 1 has nine 80,000-gallon fermenters.

After fresh yeast is added, fermentation begins. A whiskey enthusiast can probably tell you what the mash bill is on all his favorite whiskeys because a percentage of corn is a simple thing to understand. However, the influence of a microorganism like yeast is harder to explain. For that reason, yeast is arguably the single most overlooked part of what makes Jack Daniel's (or any whiskey) taste the way it does. In the days of Jess Gamble or Lem Tolley, samples of that yeast were drawn from the day's work and stored in a yeast jug, usually made from copper. The Master Distiller would take that jug home with him every day for safekeeping, ensuring the survival of the house yeast strain in the event of an accident.

The problem with jug yeast is that what the distiller preserves is actually the descendant of the yeast used that day. So, the yeast Frank Bobo used at the end of his long tenure was not a perfect copy of the yeast cultivated by Jess Motlow for the distillery's 1938 revival, but a close relative. By moving to lab-grown yeast, the distillery has arrested any drift that may have been taking place in the yeast strain. All yeast used in the fermenters is periodically and regularly grown from the stock sample, and that sample is never exposed to the environment outside the lab. The Jack Daniel's laboratory employs one microbiologist for the dedicated purpose of yeast and lactic culture. Nowadays, reserve strains are kept both on- and off-site in cryogenic storage, rather than in the Master Distiller's refrigerator. That yeast is then propagated in a mash house wholly separate from the one visitors see. Grown in mashes of rye and barley (the corn is cooked at such high temperature it would kill the yeast), up to 1,700 gallons of the stuff is used per fermentation.

Whether it be at a winery, brewery, or even on a pile of slightly rotten fruit in the tropics, it's the yeast that makes the alcohol. That process is what causes the vats of mash to bubble, and that bubbling is mostly carbon dioxide. Fermentation also produces heat, and too much heat will kill the yeast and stop fermentation in its tracks. In Jack Daniel's day, that heat excluded fermentation from the summer months, as cooling was taken care of by the open air. That is the origin of the "summer shutdown," when a distillery ceases operations and does all its major routine maintenance work. In today's Cave Spring Hollow, cooling is managed by running water through coils at the bottom of the fermenter.

In Lynchburg, mash cooking and fermentation both take place inside large stainless steel vats. Most of the vats are tucked away underneath the steel grill floor, with only the tops above the floor and approachable. Visitors to Lynchburg who let their minds wander on the tour could be forgiven for confusing the two stages, but a visual cue distinguishes a cooker from a fermenter at JD 1: the fermenters have lids. The carbon dioxide released during fermentation

Fermenter
# 16
FERMENTER
Nº16

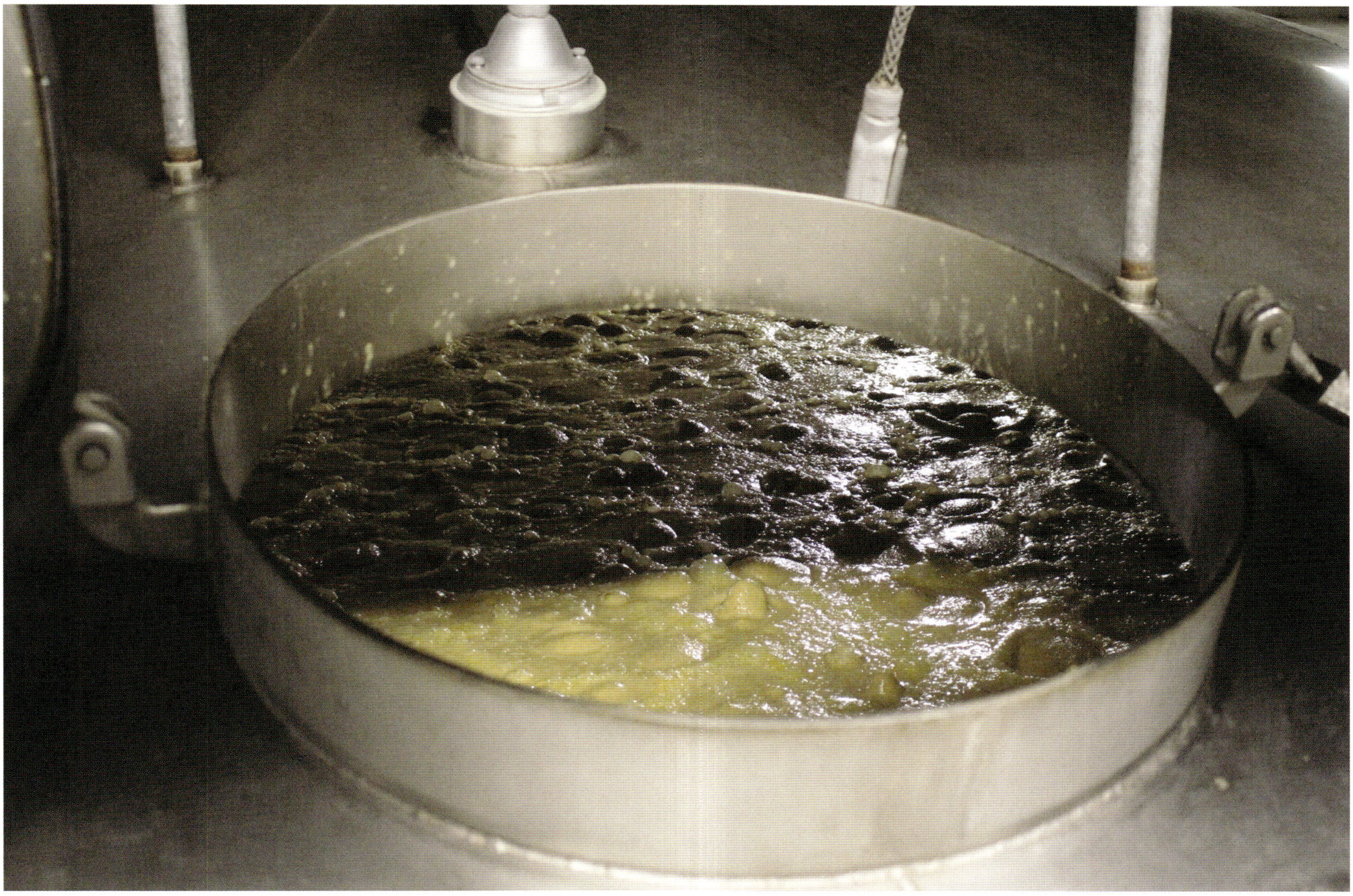

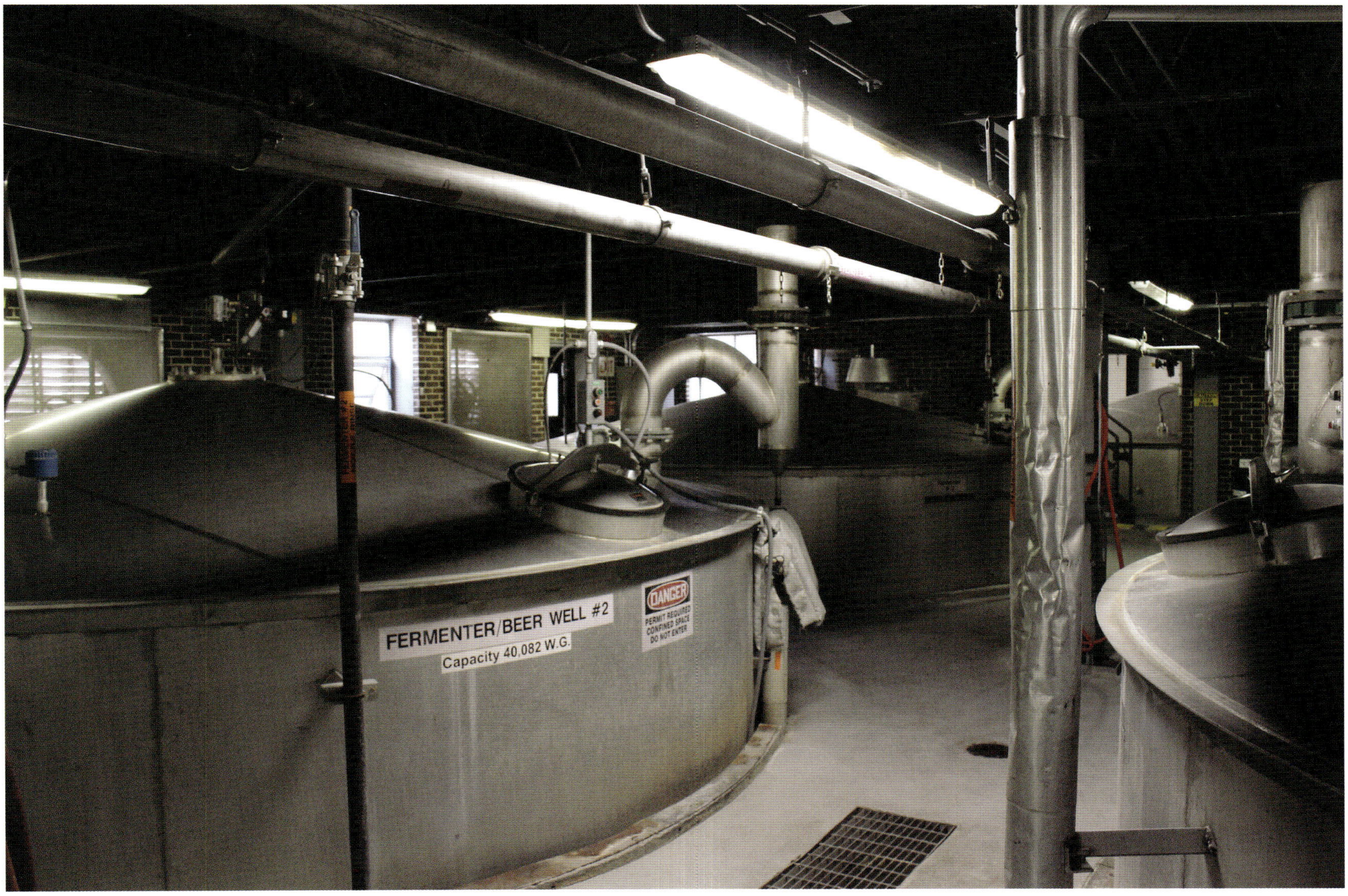
FERMENTER/BEER WELL #2
Capacity 40,082 W.G.
DANGER
PERMIT REQUIRED
CONFINED SPACE
DO NOT ENTER

FACTURED BY
dome,
COPPER
RASS WORKS
ORPORATED

# Do Old Forester and Jack Daniel's Use the Same Yeast?

A curiosity among the most observant whiskey enthusiasts is a similarity between Jack Daniel's and their Brown-Forman stablemate, Old Forester. Both have a prominent banana note, and although that note is more pronounced and (and thus more often observed) in Jack Daniel's whiskeys, the scent and flavor of bananas is widely noted in both brands. With some knowledgeable observers drawing this parallel—and since that banana flavor comes from fermentation—a few have posed the insightful question: Is there something going on with the yeast? Could the two strains be cousins, either by accident or design?

"Those yeast strains are very different," said Chris Fletcher. Long before he came home to Lynchburg, Fletcher spent eight years working in the Brown-Forman lab. "Even though I wasn't a microbiologist, I pretended to be one when I was in the Brown-Forman lab. So those two strains are very different."

Still, Fletcher can see why that line between JD and Old Forester whiskey gets drawn, and even has his own opinion on those banana notes. "Old Forester is more tropical and darker. For me, Jack Daniel's is fresher."

So, the banana flavor does not come from the yeast strains used in the two whiskeys, as is sometimes guessed at. However, there is a commonality. "Some of that really goes back to the reliance on malted barley enzymes," said Fletcher. "How [the yeast is] being fed in fermentation is identical. That is a significant difference outside this company."

The folks who have wondered about that similar note are onto something. It is not the yeast strains, however, that are the commonality. The similarity is in how those two very independent yeasts are employed in fermentation. It could be said that beyond the Jack Daniel's way of making whiskey, distinctive as it is, are some features of how Brown-Forman makes whiskey generally.

would become dangerous to workers if allowed to build up in the fermentation room. Although some distilleries have open-topped fermentation vats, those buildings are very well-ventilated, and JD 1 is not. The solution was to put a lid on the fermenter, contain the carbon dioxide, and vent it directly from the source. Should you visit, beware of a popular prank associated with fermenters of this kind: a tour guide might invite you to smell a fermenter and open the lid for you, whereupon the hot, concentrated carbon dioxide will give your nostrils a mild burning sensation. It's not harmful, but it does supply a bit of a shock.

A fermentation run in Lynchburg lasts for between four and six days, for an average of 100 hours—a full extra day beyond the 72-hour average which is typical of the wider bourbon industry (although it should be noted some major Kentucky distilleries ferment, on average, well beyond 100 hours). An extended fermentation time allows for more flavor to develop, whereas a shorter period is about maximizing efficiency in alcohol production. When a Jack Daniel's fermentation run is over, they have a distiller's beer with about 12 percent alcohol by volume (ABV). This distiller's beer, already endowed with the alcoholic strength of a glass of wine, is ready to be piped off to distillation. The rule of thumb at the distillery is that five gallons of distiller's beer translates into one gallon of new make whiskey.

## Copper

As is the case with all major distilleries in America, Jack Daniel's relies on an American variant of the column still, sometimes referred to as a beer still. This design is centered on a single column, which is where it differs from its cousins in most other spirits industries, which utilize two or more columns.

Distillation takes advantage of the differing boiling points of liquids, which are leveraged to concentrate one of them. If the liquid can be heated to the right temperature, the selected component can be vaporized out of it. In the case of spiritous liquors, distillation relies on alcohol having a substantially lower boiling point (173.1°F) than water (212°F). Steam is pumped into the base of the still, and the boozy wash from the fermenter is pumped into a point near the middle. The steam rises to meet the wash as it comes down the still, causing the alcohol and other compounds to separate from the water in the wash. Each plate causes that part of the still to function like its own mini still, as each successive plate going up the column is cooler than the one beneath it. The vapors in the still partially condense in each chamber and fall onto the plate, where they vaporize again. The heavier volatile elements (congeners, acids, esters, etc.) each have their own boiling points, so each separates out at a different part of the still. A portion of these elements will always rise up the column with the alcohol vapor. As the vapor rises, it becomes increasingly pure. Eventually the alcohol-rich vapor is drawn out at the top, so that hot vapor can condense into a liquid called a low wine.

The low wine then goes on to the second part of the still, which at Jack Daniel's is a thumper. Or rather it would be called a thumper, except in Lynchburg "nobody calls it a thumper," said Fletcher. A thumper works by filling a small pot with low wine, and that pot sits inside a keg. Hot alcohol vapor from the column still floods into the keg, transferring heat to it and the low wine inside. That vaporizes the contents of the pot, activating the second round of distillation necessary to make it into high wines. The heat transfer also cools off the alcohol vapor coming from the column still, causing it to condense, whereupon it is collected from the keg and fed into the pot.

The mechanism is very energy efficient, and the pressure buildup inside causes a loud popping noise, hence the name "thumper." An idiosyncrasy of Lynchburg's equipment is that it makes no audible noise.

The American system departs from the one used in Ireland, Scotland, and most of Japan, because the second half for those industries is another column, not a thumper or a doubler. In the US, if a thumper isn't used, an alternate mechanism called a doubler (basically a pot still) is utilized in its place. Americans want a heavier, more flavorful new make whiskey, so it doesn't need the raw purity achieved by a distillation run through a second, matching column.

Visitors to the distillery can see both the low wines and high wines coming off the works in the pair's glass-paneled copper boxes that sit adjacent to the five stills in JD 1. When their respective stills are in operation, the funnels in these boxes gush with clear liquid, even the low wines heavy with alcohol. At Jack Daniel's, the desired strength of the fresh off the still, new make whiskey is 140 proof, which is fairly typical in the wider bourbon industry. The legal maximum is 160 proof, but hardly anyone distills to above 140 proof. This is because the higher the proof off the still, the fewer native flavors from fermentation make it into the whiskey. Some whiskey producers in America distill to as low as 110 proof, maximizing the native flavor aspect, but 140 has become the favored balance struck between flavor and producing plenty of alcohol.

Unlike a pot still, which runs individual batches of wash, a column still like the units used at Jack Daniel's see wash continuously pumped in and low wines continuously drawn out. The doubler also runs continuously, since what goes in is truly all liquid. This is why the process is referred to as "continuous distillation" and partially why column stills are more efficient and have seen such widespread adoption in the whiskey industry, especially among distillers requiring large-scale production. In Dan Call's day, their needs could still be

STILL
Nº5
61,714.3 wg

JACK DANIEL'S
Old No. 7 Brand
Barbour

# Lexie Phillips

For the keen observer, when Chris Fletcher was bumped up to become Jeff Arnett's successor in October 2020, the question became who would take Fletcher's place as the Assistant Master Distiller. That announcement came five months later when Brown-Forman announced that Jack Daniel's would see its first woman serving in so senior a position in the still house.

Phillips was born and raised near Lynchburg and is an example of the distillery's multigenerational workforce. She is a fourth-generation employee and is said to have dozens (with an "s") of relatives who either are working or have worked for Jack Daniel's. For her education, Phillips started at Motlow State Community College before transferring to Middle Tennessee State University (MTSU) in Murfreesboro, where she earned her degree in agricultural science in 2012. She points back to Professor Tony Johnston at MTSU as being one of the seminal influences that directed her to the whiskey industry. Johnston would later become the director of MTSU's Fermentation Science program.

Phillips was hired at Jack Daniel's in 2014, rising to distillery lead operator before the appointment as Assistant Master Distiller. Over those seven years, she was one of the key players in developing Jack Daniel's Tennessee Rye, which has since evolved into the Jack Daniel's Bonded Rye.

Nowadays, anyone with the words "master distiller" in their job title is also expected to function as a brand ambassador. Phillips moved into that role in the midst of the COVID-19 pandemic, so hitting the road and supporting the company's storytelling was delayed. And at the time of writing, Phillips had fully stepped back from ambassadorial duties. "Her passion is turning corn into whiskey," said her boss, Chris Fletcher. "She wants to make whiskey, and not talk about making whiskey. So, now she is focused 100 percent on the stillhouse." Even so, this was a time of new projects, such as taking part in the launch of the Jack Daniel's 10 Year Old.

In an interview for *Success* magazine, Phillips describes that part of the job in these terms: "That was my dream. I became the sixth whiskey-making woman—as a distillery operator—to ever work at Jack Daniel's. People think it's a boys' club, but that's not the case at all. The work is hard manual labor, and just one of those things that not a lot of women want to do."

Prognostication can be a punishing exercise, but Phillips's place has some interesting features worth taking notice of. Both her and Fletcher are relatively young to occupy the top production and quality control spots at a major American whiskey distillery: as I write this, Fletcher is 43 and Phillips is in her middle 30s. Unless Fletcher's future holds a promotion to a more senior executive position, we can expect his tenure as Master Distiller to last into the 2040s. Fletcher himself started out at Jack Daniel's working as a lowly tour guide, later moving on to other jobs in the whiskey industry before returning home. Perhaps Phillips will also venture away from Lynchburg before returning?

As it is, Phillips is part of the growing presence of women in the whiskey trade. Focusing on her own immediate professional environs, just a dozen miles away in Tullahoma is Tennessee's second-biggest distillery in Cascade Hollow (aka George Dickel), where Nicole Austin has been Master Distiller since 2018. Within Jack Daniel's parent company of Brown-Forman, after years of working as Chris Morris's deputy, Elizabeth McCall succeeded him as Master Distiller at Woodford Reserve in 2023. In blazing some new trails in Lynchburg, Phillips is joining a growing phalanx of whiskey-making women, and, in her case, working for one of the industry's biggest names.

met with pot stills, even though column still technology had been patented as early as 1830. Modern pot still spirits production is either small in scale, such as with craft distillers, or utilizes one or more sets of large pot stills, as is the case in Scotland and Ireland.

Another point of efficiency is that column stills are extremely effective at simplifying the removal of the inferior and unwanted alcohols in the wash, known as the *foreshots*, *heads*, and *tails*. The foreshot, for example, contains the toxic compounds that blind or even kill those who drink it. These can be automatically vented straight out of the column still, whereas in a pot still they must be cut from the still run at the beginning and end of the process.

In theory, if a column still has enough plates inside it, it can create an almost pure alcohol vapor entirely in one mechanism. In practice, that would make for an unwieldy contraption, which is why grain whisky stills in Scotland or Japan use two columns, and a vodka column still might use as many as four or five columns. Meanwhile, the output potential of a column still can be estimated by its width. Thus, how the design of a column still works is deceptively simple, with the desired characteristics of the low wine coming out of a Jack Daniel's still governed by how many plates, how those plates are perforated (i.e., how many and how large are the holes in each plate), and how far apart those plates are in the still. The potential output is governed by the width. Two column stills fabricated to slightly different specifications can produce markedly different distillates.

This is why when an expansion of production capacity is required at a major distillery, the existing stills are duplicated exactly, as happened at Jack Daniel's. JD 1 comes equipped with two large stills of 76 inches diameter and two smaller stills of 54 inches diameter. Regardless of width, all four stills are 45 feet tall and have 18 plates. The big stills can produce 225 gallons of new make per minute, while the small stills manage 90 gallons per minute. When Brown-Forman decided to expand production and built JD 2, it copied the small, 54-inch still design and installed two of them in the new stillhouse. "JD 2 has one-fifth the output of JD 1," said Jeff Arnett. "When I left, total output was 55 million proof gallons per year."

All the stills used at Jack Daniel's are built and maintained by Vendome Copper & Brass Works in Louisville, Kentucky, the premier still fabricators for America's whiskey industry. They are made from copper, the most desired metal for stills, so much so that even stills fashioned primarily from stainless steel are almost always made with some copper parts inside them. The primary reason for using copper is that it reacts with certain unwanted trace chemicals in the vapor, such as sulfur compounds, and removes them. The metal is also an excellent conductor of heat, making it useful for a giant controlled vaporization machine like a still.

## Charcoal

After leaving the stills, the new make whiskey goes onto the next step, the one that separates Tennessee Whiskey from Tennessee bourbon—the Lincoln County Process. State law describes it as filtration of new make whiskey through sugar maple charcoal prior to barreling. This system is also applied to Jack Daniel's rye and malt whiskeys, even though there is no legal requirement for those offerings. The Lincoln County Process and the way Jack Daniel's carries it out is very much the distillery's signature.

In Lynchburg, the new make whiskey is run through a perforated pipe running across the top of a vat packed with 10 solid feet of crushed charcoal. The whiskey drips on the charcoal, soaks it, and saturation plus gravity does the rest, leading to a steady stream of filtered whiskey coming out the bottom of the vat.

Anyone who has ever owned a Brita pitcher is already at least vaguely familiar with what charcoal does. Carbon is a chemically "sticky" element—other compounds tend to bind with it. This feature is what makes it ideal for use in filters, and according to the UN Food and Agriculture Organization, hardwood charcoal is between 70 and 80 percent carbon.

What exactly the Jack Daniel's method of charcoal mellowing does to their own new make whiskey is a trade secret, but how the process works in general terms was confirmed by John P. Munafo in a 2019 study for the University of Tennessee Institute of Agriculture. Using samples provided by Sugarlands Distilling Company in Gatlinburg, Munafo and his graduate assistant identified all the aroma-causing compounds in the new make whiskey, and then measured them before and after application of charcoal mellowing. All of the aroma-causing agents were reduced, some only marginally and some by as much as 50 percent. Munafo's study found that the greatest reductions were seen in compounds identified as producing undesirable "malty, rancid, fatty, and roasty aromas." At the distillery, they call these unwanted flavor elements the "cooked corn cereal oil notes."

Since the American craft distilling movement began in earnest after 2005, small distillers around the country have been looking for a means to shorten the necessary years needed to produce a properly mature whiskey. Keeping that in mind, I have come to see charcoal mellowing as the original shortcut, because reducing these noxious volatile compounds before maturation has even begun produces a smoother whiskey in less time. Although peer bourbons from Jim Beam and Evan Williams are of similar age, Jack Daniel's Old No. 7 is undeniably mellower.

The most common misunderstanding about the Lincoln County Process is that it *imparts* flavors into the new whiskey. Some folks perceive a maple note in the whiskey, which they are taking from the sugar maple charcoal. Yet sugar maple was not chosen for any flavor qualities, nor does the charcoal impart any. Making charcoal requires prolonged exposure to temperatures above 750°F, and anyone who has ever seen the charcoal being made at Jack Daniel's is already familiar with the intense heat of that blaze, which peaks at over 2,000°F. Sugar burns at just 350°F, and burnt sugar quickly turns bitter. Whereas an oak bourbon barrel is briefly scorched on the inside, charcoal is thoroughly burnt and roasted, deeply carbonizing it. Little to none of the maple's sugars remain by the time it is sitting in a vat at the Jack Daniel's Distillery. The process is entirely about removing unwanted flavors, not adding them.

I have asked both Jeff Arnett and Chris Fletcher about why sugar maple is used, and their answers were the same: it is a cheap, abundant hardwood in Tennessee. Also, Tennessee doesn't have the climate for a profitable maple syrup industry, leaving a lot of sugar maples available.

CHARCOAL

PRODUCTION

We Don't Measure
Wood At These Times
Before 8:00 2:00-2:15
9:00-9:15 After 3:00
11:30-12:00 SAT. or Sun.

CAT
CAT

The Jack Daniel's Distillery has a huge appetite for charcoal, only exceeded by its truly vast appetite for corn. In a long, single-story building (a series of connected buildings, really) next to JD 1 sit 72 charcoal vats, most made from wood (some are stainless steel). JD 2 has 14 more. A batch of charcoal in each may last for four to six months, but with 86 vats in total and each requiring 10 feet of packed charcoal, making that charcoal is a regular part of the grind at the distillery.

The charcoal is made on-site at the distillery rickyard, found uphill from Cave Spring, in a specialized pavilion somewhat reminiscent of a pagoda. The heavily built, fireproof structure has two burn stations, each one open around the sides and vented through a common chimney in the roof. That roof provides some shelter from the elements, allowing charcoal burns to take place in the rain.

In its modern context, Jack Daniel's has been sourcing at least some of its sugar maple since the late 1940s. The days when a Motlow boy would apprentice in the family business by chopping down sugar maple trees during the winter months while burning last year's felled timber for charcoal are a historical footnote. Some of the sawmills that provide sugar maple staves for Jack Daniel's have been doing business with the distillery for several decades, and most of them are local. "They are mostly in Tennessee," said Chris Fletcher. "A few are in spots north of Nashville."

Staves of dried sugar maple are stacked up, leaving plenty of space between the staves for ventilation. One such five-foot stack makes a pallet, and two pallets are placed next to each other in a burn (where they tend to collapse into each other). The fire is started between them, using a can of new make whiskey as the accelerant. A burn can take as long as two hours, but once ready, the pile of burning charcoal is raked and turned over with a small bulldozer and doused with water. Once extinguished, it is moved just across the yard to a grinder, which crushes the charcoal between steel rollers to a more or less uniform size. One burn fills one pan with charcoal and, according to Jeff Arnett, four pans are needed to fill a vat. Normally the distillery will see three charcoal burns per day, three days per week.

“Staves of dried sugar maple are stacked up, leaving plenty of space between the staves for ventilation. One such five-foot stack makes a pallet, and two pallets are placed next to each other in a burn (where they tend to collapse into each other).”

WHISKEY FOR
DESTRUCTION

“A burn can take as long as two hours, but once ready, the pile of burning charcoal is raked and turned over with a small bulldozer and doused with water.”

CHARCOAL MELLOWING
VAT-NO.50
CAP.2872 W.G.

MELLOWING
VAT 36

"A batch of charcoal in each may last for four to six months, but with 86 vats in total and each requiring 10 feet of packed charcoal, making that charcoal is a regular part of the grind at the distillery."

JACK DANIEL'S

# Jeff Arnett

Ironically, as a young man Jeff Arnett never set out to pursue a career making whiskey or even a career in the broader world of manufacturing food and drink. Arnett wanted to apply his engineering degree to a career in the automotive industry. He started out at the University of Tennessee at Martin, doing a co-op with Allied Signal/Bendix Brakes while there. To finish a four-year degree, he transferred to the University of Alabama, where upon graduation he discovered that car-making was a troubled industry. Arnett recalled how "that year, GM laid off about 3,000 people," and engineering jobs in the business were scarce.

The folks who were hiring were Proctor & Gamble, the biggest employer in Arnett's hometown of Jackson, Tennessee, at the time. But as it turned out, they were not hiring in Jackson. Instead, they invited Arnett to apply for a job at their Folgers Coffee plant in New Orleans, the largest of the Folgers plants and probably the largest coffee-making facility in the country at that time. After learning sensory science and the coffee business there—working on the development of Folgers Singles along the way—he went on to work on Sunny Delight orange drink. Finally, he headed back to the Proctor & Gamble plant in his hometown to work on Pringles potato chips. However, Proctor & Gamble was getting out of the food business, so after a decade with the company, Arnett was offered a choice of voluntary separation or taking a risk by following Pringles into the hands of another corporation.

After he decided to leave Proctor & Gamble, Arnett's first choice was to return to his original dream job: engineering in the auto industry. In a twist of fate, Arnett's headhunter told him that a major beverage company in Nashville was looking for talent. Thinking it had to be Coca-Cola or Pepsi or something similar, Arnett pressed for something from Nissan, until his headhunter finally told him the beverage company was Jack Daniel's. Arnett's initial response was in the vein of "Why did you say Nashville, because Jack Daniel's is in Lynchburg?" Arnett was already a Squire, having been nominated by his father, and, as a native Tennessean, was (and remains) proud of Jack Daniel's. Eventually he interviewed with Jack Daniel's, an experience that firmly sold him on the idea of working there. Arnett was hired in May 2001.

Arnett's start was an interesting one. My experience has been that most people who become a Chief Blender or Chief Distiller for a major whiskey company often start their careers outside the industry but move over into at least making spirits after just a few years. Arnett came over much later but made up for the lost time by learning and rising fast. This he partially credits to working in quality control, which he describes as one of the very few tasks at Jack Daniel's that involves having a toe in all parts of the production process, from grain to barrel dumping to shipping cases. It's a view his successor, Chris Fletcher, generally shares, as Fletcher has described one of his primary roles as chief quality controller. Nowadays it is even written into the Master Distiller's formal job title, as Director of Quality.

Seven years later, he was offered the Master Distiller's job. Arnett has said that Jimmy Bedford was already looking at retirement before the sexual harassment incident forced him out. There was no heir apparent, so the search for a successor began. Arnett, perhaps unknowingly, helped himself when he took over the single barrel program. Bedford had started that, and his affection for it was part of what drove Bedford to travel as much as he did. While he was out selling it, Arnett was put in position to know what was going on in terms of the product's development. Arnett also knew as much as anyone at the distillery about affairs at the distillery in general due to his role in quality control.

Other projects Arnett took on during this time elevated his stature. About two years before Bedford was asked to resign, Arnett led a media tour that impressed Mike Keyes, who would become the president of Brown-Forman's North American division. Keyes put him on the short list as a potential Bedford successor.

"I was actually shocked when I was chosen," said Arnett. It was an excellent opportunity, but Arnett had two small children at home, and therefore no desire to travel as much as Bedford did. "We eventually agreed on 20 percent travel," said Arnett, which in practice meant spending 50 to 60 days a year on the road. Most of that was international, because Arnett's tenure saw continued market growth overseas. "When I started in 2001, Jack Daniel's was in 120 countries, and by the time I left, it was like 170." For the record, the United Nations recognizes 193 nation-states today. The period also saw the company's first major production infrastructure expansion since the 1960s, when Jack Daniel's No. 2 was built in the middle of the 2010s.

Change in Lynchburg marked the Arnett period, with Jack Daniel's adding eight regular expressions to its lineup. In the 1990s and 2000s, the decades when the foundations of the Bourbon Boom were being built up, Jack Daniel's was perceived as being staid by most whiskey enthusiasts. Old No. 7 has always had its own devoted fan base, but this was largely separate from the world of whiskey lovers. Thus, Jack Daniel's was late to the game in developing new expressions in the way other whiskey companies were. In describing the attitude then, Arnett says, "There wasn't interest in that, and Jack Daniel's didn't need it to grow."

It's worth recalling that Jack Daniel's entered the 1980s with just Old No. 7 Black Label, plus the much more modestly distributed Lem Motlow Sour Mash and Jack Daniel's Green Label. The latter two had become mere curiosities by the late twentieth century. The 1980s saw just one new expression introduced, Gentleman Jack; the 1990s saw one more, Jack Daniel's Single Barrel. So, there were some stubborn attitudes to overcome within the company in regard to introducing new expressions, even though all of the other major American whiskey distillers were having success. "It took me five years to convince them to do Cask Strength Single Barrel," said Arnett. "A lot of sacred cows fell during that time."

Despite joining the party late, what Arnett brought to it mattered: turning Single Barrel into an expansive line all its own, introducing rye whiskey (with Lynchburg's first new mash bill since the nineteenth century), and bringing Bottled in Bond to Jack Daniel's. All the new products caused some whiskey enthusiasts who had previously scoffed at Mr. Jack's whiskey to give it a second look, bringing in new fans. Arnett Is most proud of all of the awards Heritage Barrel won, as well as the now discontinued No. 27 Gold, despite all the problems that came with aging in maple barrels.

By the time the introduction of the new expressions was in full swing, Arnett had become one of the luminaries of the trade, and not just with whiskey enthusiasts or Jack Daniel's fans. "I moved back to Lynchburg to work for Jeff. Period," said Chris Fletcher, who eventually became Arnett's successor. "He really allowed me to push innovation and [also] create that Assistant Master Distiller role. He's one of my favorite people in the world."

Serving as Master Distiller (or Blender) at a major whiskey company would be the pinnacle of a career for some. The most revered names in the industry are those who spent decades at that peak, using it to shape the core identity of the whiskeys they made. After 20 years in Lynchburg, a dozen of them in the top job, Arnett felt differently. He wanted the peak of his career to be making something of his own and for himself. With a well-prepared successor, Chris Fletcher, waiting in the wings, Arnett announced his retirement from Jack Daniel's in 2020.

Joining with a handful of veterans from Tennessee's craft distilling sector, Arnett cofounded the curiously named Company Distilling (the "company" part refers to good company, not the business enterprise meaning). It's not quite a start-up, as the venture absorbed the H. Clark Distillery in Thompson's Station, but it still presents all the challenges that a start-up whiskey company would. Some may look at it as a step down from Jack Daniel's, but not Arnett. Company Distilling is undoubtedly smaller, but it's something he has a stake in, and with that comes more freedom to innovate. Arnett remains proud of his work at Jack Daniel's, but he looks at having something he can call his own as his real legacy.

## Oak

Once filtered, the new make whiskey is ready for the barrel. By law, the whiskey filling the barrel cannot exceed 125 proof, and that maximum is the standard barrel entry proof used by Jack Daniel's. Recall that the new make is distilled to 140 proof, so even that maximum requires the whiskey to be watered down some. This is done with water from Cave Spring, although that water is filtered to food safety standards for this purpose.

Note that 125 proof is the standard, because the distillery has exceptions. Jack Daniel's Heritage Barrel uses the much lower entry proof of 100. The reason that lower entry proof matters for a premium whiskey like Heritage Barrel illustrates why entry proof matters in general, which in turn is why aging in charred new oak barrels is a crucial feature not just of Jack Daniel's whiskey, but American whiskeys generally.

In the wider bourbon industry, new oak maturation is said to account for between 50 and 85 percent of how a whiskey tastes and smells, depending on which distillery is doing the talking and how long that whiskey is aged. Barrel aging also contributes 100 percent of the color. The barrels used at Jack Daniel's, with few exceptions, are American Standard Barrels, a class of 53-gallon containers fashioned from *Quercus alba*, or white oak. The exceptions include the various spent casks from the wine industry or other spirits industries used for secondary maturation ("finishing"); new white oak casks made in a specialized way, such as those used in making Jack Daniel's Sinatra Select; and highly exotic casks made from unusual wood choices, such as the maple casks used to make the Jack Daniel's No. 27 Gold Edition.

The typical Jack Daniel's barrel is fashioned from oak that has seen a minimum of six months of air drying. After the body of the barrel is fashioned from the staves, the first preparatory step is toasting. The interior of the barrel is exposed to less heat than in the later step of charring—around 500°F or 550°F—but for a much longer period of time. For Jack Daniel's barrels, toasting lasts for 13 minutes. The process expresses the lactones and breaks down the cellulose in the oak more fully than charring, producing more wood flavor in the vein of caramel, coconut, and vanilla.

Jack Daniel's is unusual for just how much they lean on their toasting. "We hang our hats on that," said Master Distiller Chris Fletcher. Some of the peers of Jack Daniel's in the Kentucky bourbon industry rely solely on charring, and while others both toast and char barrels, the toasting period preferred in Lynchburg is particularly long. Over at their Brown-Forman stablemate Woodford Reserve, Master Distiller Elizabeth McCall has said they toast their barrels for only 10 minutes. Jeff Arnett once stated the long toasting practice was adapted from the wine industry, back during a period when Brown-Forman had a lot of wine in its corporate portfolio.

Next the barrel is charred, as required by federal law. This is the most famous part of making a barrel, which sees the insides set on fire. The wider industry describes charring in terms of four levels, with each level indicating how long the burn is allowed to go on. Level IV is the highest, indicating a 55-second burn. At Jack Daniel's, the standard barrel receives between 20 and 25 seconds of charring, which lands between Level I and II. In the barrel-making industry, Level II char is considered a "finish the barrel" setting. Although most of the Kentucky bourbon industry prefers Level III and IV, Jack Daniel's preference for their lower, custom char makes sense after their prolonged toasting period. Raising the char from Level II to III is an increase from 30 to a mere 35 seconds burn time, but in those five seconds much or all of the coconut flavor would be scorched. After toasting and charring, the barrel heads are put on and the cooper's work is done.

After the barrels are filled, they are transported to one of Jack Daniel's 95 rickhouses, most of which are located in Moore County, but the company's storage and aging complex has expanded in recent years into neighboring Lincoln County. The rickhouse, or "rack for tiering barrels," was patented by Frederick Stitzel in 1879. This is a (often multi-floor) system of racks that allows for both efficient storage of barrels and for good ventilation around the barrels and throughout the building. It is best to think of a rickhouse as free-standing rows of racks, with a simple cladded exterior. When one considers that 40,000 full barrels of whiskey weighs 11,000 tons, any structure capable of bearing that load plus its own weight can easily handle the walls and roof. That exterior stuff is just small change for a big rickhouse. The smallest rickhouses are modest affairs, storing 6,000 barrels, while the largest stand eight stories and hold well over 50,000 barrels.

Clay
JACK DANIEL

BARREL HOUSE

JACK DANIEL DISTILLERY
No 1

# For Jack Daniel's, Fire Is Serious Business

For decades, Jack Daniel's was the only distillery in the world to have its own fire department. Sometimes, this is confused and downplayed, as Brown-Forman supports the Moore County Fire Department. But no, an independent, company-operated fire brigade is stationed on the same property as the bottling plant and a cluster of rickhouses, two miles southwest of the distillery proper. Nowadays, other big distillers, such as Jim Beam, have their own in-house fire and emergency response teams, but Jack Daniel's establishment remains the most substantial.

The distillery's in-house fire brigade dates back to its restoration in 1937 and 1938. Lem Motlow had some previous experience with distillery fires and decided to address the issue directly. Tourists visiting the distillery can see two of the antique fire engines on display, between the yard where charcoal for the Lincoln County Process is made and Cave Spring. These vehicles are brought out for parades in Lynchburg, but are otherwise very much retired.

The Jack Daniel's No. 7 Fire Brigade began with Motlow's concerns, but the major influence on the modern brigade was the disastrous 1996 fire that befell Heaven Hill, the Kentucky bourbon company that (at that time) was centered in Bardstown. The blaze was carried to the stillhouse and several other rickhouses, destroying much of Heaven Hill's plant and aging whiskey stock. Reports say between 100 and 125 firefighters turned out to combat the alcohol-fueled inferno. But as literal burning rivers of whiskey flowed down access roads and hillsides, they could do little more than contain the blaze.

The disaster was influential throughout the American whiskey industry, prompting the enactment of new safety requirements and procedures, but Heaven Hill's catastrophe cast a shadow onto more than just fire safety codes. To make good on the loss of their stillhouse and much of their bourbon stocks, Heaven Hill ultimately bought Bernheim in Shively, Kentucky (an industrial suburb of Louisville), splitting the company's operations between two places about 40 miles apart. Heaven Hill also purchased aged whiskey from other bourbon companies to bridge the gap in their stocks and production. Brown-Forman, which also owns Old Forester and Woodford Reserve, was one of them.

The way everyone in mid-1990s Kentucky bourbon stepped up to support Heaven Hill is a moment the industry as a whole remains proud of, but it must have made anyone in the business of risk calculation at Brown-Forman especially nervous. Heaven Hill could find replacement stocks of bourbon and acquire an alternate distillery rather than build one from scratch. If a similar calamity had befallen Jack Daniel's, they would have absolutely needed to rebuild from nothing, while the only possible source of replacement Tennessee Whiskey was the much smaller George Dickel. A Heaven Hill–scale fire in Lynchburg could doom the company, so, in addition to the code changes that impacted how rickhouses were situated and protected from fire, the No. 7 Fire Brigade saw expansions and upgrades, as well.

Today, the Jack Daniel's fire department consists of just shy of three dozen members. All are volunteers and employees at the company. At any given time, a handful are on duty at the firehouse, while most are doing their main jobs at the distillery. In the event of an emergency call, whoever is a member of the brigade and at work is mobilized off their primary job and onto emergency response. As a fire brigade, they are specialized in dealing with distillery-specific hazards, and thus all their firefighting equipment is built around foam and dry chemicals. Underscoring just how much whiskey is kept in the estimated 2 million barrels stored on various Jack Daniel's properties: the No. 7 Fire Brigade stocks more foam than any airport east of the Mississippi.

That Jack Daniel's has its own fire department accomplishes more than safeguard the future of the distillery and its whiskey, although that is its undoubted purpose. The brigade also has mutual support agreements with local emergency services. While that does mean Daniel's can call for help from county fire departments, the distillery has never suffered a serious fire. In practice, it is more likely that No. 7 Fire Brigade is the one being called upon for support away from the distillery grounds.

JACK DANIEL'S
FIRE BRIGADE
LYNCHBURG
TN

JACK DANIEL'S
Tennessee
FIRE
EASTERN US CHAMPIONSHIP
CMSA
MURFREESBORO, TN

JACK DANIEL'S
ENGINE CO.
1

Contrary to the notion whiskey fans often hold "that older is always better," some of the least-productive rickhouses owned by Jack Daniel's are their oldest and smallest. "Our worst performing barrel house today was built by Lem [Motlow]," said Eddy.

Once racked up in the rickhouse, most barrels will not be moved until they are matured and ready for dumping, and where a barrel is racked up decides much of how that maturation plays out. Because the rickhouse is designed with air circulation in mind, the warmer, lighter, and drier air rises while the cooler, damper, and heavier air sinks to the bottom. Rickhouses commonly have depressed cavities in their floors, allowing the coldest air to sink below the barrels. Sometimes the windows are opened to improve air circulation, especially on the upper floors and during the summer months. Air circulation is the sole climate controller inside the building, so the overall temperature will rise and fall with the seasons, and during the course of a year in Moore County it is typical to see lows of below 20°F during winter and humid summer peaks of over 100°F. Inside a rickhouse during summer, the ground floor is usually quite pleasant, but the temperature can climb by as much as 15 degrees with each floor, so that the top floor is roasting. During winter, the ground floor will be quite frigid, while the top floor might be warm enough to force workers to doff their coats.

This effect is important (and justifies the expense of building a rickhouse instead of stacking the barrels up on pallets). The sweltering summer drives the whiskey into the barrel's wood, while the cold winters pull it back out. The barrel is a breathable container that interacts with the air constantly moving around it, which drives the chemistry of maturation.

First, the charred interior of the barrel offers a second round of charcoal filtration, but this is quite modest compared to what happened during charcoal mellowing. As it is driven into the wood by the summer heat, the whiskey absorbs flavors such as sweet vanilla and bitter tannins, and these flavors are pulled back out of the wood with the liquid during the winter.

Because the barrel is breathable, its contents evaporate over time. This process is better known as the "Angel's Share," and those angels demand different tolls, depending on where the barrel was lodged in the rickhouse. On the dry upper floors of the rickhouse, the lack of moisture pulls more water vapor out of the barrel, causing the proof of the whiskey to rise. On the lower floors, the relatively damp conditions ensure that it is the alcohol that evaporates at a faster rate. The differences in climates also drive how much of a share the angels claim; at Jack Daniel's, the top floors favored for selecting Single Barrel whiskeys could lose up to 30 percent of the whiskey by the time the barrel is dumped, but the lower floors providing the bulk for Old No. 7 usually see just 10 percent loss.

As water and alcohol vapor leave the barrel, fresh air trickles into it, triggering other chemical reactions in the whiskey. The simplest explanation lies in how both water and alcohol are odorless and tasteless. What a whiskey tastes and smells like comes from the many trace compounds found in it. Some of the best of these elements can only form after they oxidize and break down, a process that demands time and exposure to the air. The Lincoln County Process offers one shortcut to making a smooth whiskey, while certain craft distillers have leaned heavily on other methods to extract the most flavor and color from the oak barrel as swiftly as possible. But for this last part of the process, only time will tell.

Because it eases oxidation, water is a necessary agent in breaking down some of the unwanted trace chemicals or softening the harsher flavors that come out of the barrel itself. As a rule, lower entry proof endows the whiskey with more robust flavors and a richer mouthfeel. By contrast, high entry proof is about maximizing efficiency, because putting more alcohol in the barrel saves on barrels.

The Lincoln County Process is already an expensive and inefficient step, so it is easy to understand why the company chooses to maximize efficiency with its entry proof. After all, neither Jim Beam nor Heaven Hill use charcoal mellowing, and both of them have a standard entry proof of 125. As for Heritage Barrel, its entry proof of 100 may be the lowest in regular use by any major distiller in the country. The standard entry proof at Michter's is 103, while Maker's Mark (also known for its many inefficient, idiosyncratic practices) uses an entry proof of 110.

## Oak, Coopers, and Sustainability

If a company must age every drop of whiskey in a new charred oak barrel *and* that company is the largest whiskey producer in America, they need a lot of new barrels. Masses and masses of new barrels. Note the use of the term *new*, because every single barrel needs to be new, and the process of making barrels consumes vast numbers of oak trees. Meeting that demand is a key feature of not just the Jack Daniel's production process today, but the company's strategy heading into the future as well.

When asked about just how many barrels Jack Daniel's fills in a year, Chris Fletcher spoke in general and theoretical terms. "We should fill a little less than 800,000 barrels per year, because we can't produce more proof gallons than that." A proof gallon is an industry term, defined as a liquid gallon at 60°F with 50% ABV (so half alcohol, half water). Fletcher is referring to how the distillery is running at the practical limits of its output at present.

To illustrate that figure in relative terms, when Heaven Hill announced they were building a new distillery in 2023, they indicated they were filling 450,000 barrels per year out of their existing plant, the Bernheim Distillery in Louisville. In 2021 Jim Beam declared that they had filled 1 million barrels over 18 months, which would mean an average rate of 665,000 per annum. There really is nothing quite like the scale of Jack Daniel's appetite for new oak barrels. The only other brand operating on an even larger scale, Johnnie Walker, reuses casks two, three, and sometimes even four times.

Brown-Forman acquired its first cooperage in 1946, and the company had long been proud of their in-house coopering: a mini-cooperage is the standout feature of the distillery tour at Old Forester's tourist distillery in downtown Louisville. Whenever Jack Daniel's needed a specialized barrel, such as for Sinatra Select, the company always found a way to call attention to how they made that barrel themselves. When the 2,000 to 2,500 barrel-per-day output of their Louisville cooperage was no longer sufficient to meet the demands of all of Brown-Forman's whiskey brands (Jack Daniel's, Old Forester, Woodford Reserve, etc.) they added another.

In 2014, Brown-Forman built a new cooperage in Trinity, Alabama, approximately 80 miles from Lynchburg, for the express purpose of supplying barrels to Jack Daniel's. One presumes that expansion did not work out the way Brown-Forman hoped, because by the middle of 2024 they had completed the sale of that cooperage and its associated stave mills to Independent Stave Company, a major supplier of casks to the liquor industry. When they announced the sale in February

2024, Brown-Forman stated that the Louisville cooperage was meeting half their combined demand for barrels, a clear indication that the company is outsourcing the production of hundreds of thousands of barrels per year. “Barrels are sourced from Alabama, Louisville, and other places,” said Chris Fletcher.

That Trinity experience must have truly soured someone at the Brown-Forman corporate offices on their long-held practice of vertically integrating their barrel making, because the company followed their divestment of Trinity by closing their Louisville cooperage in January 2025. They then sold it for $13.6 million that May. After decades of relying on their own people to make their barrels, Brown-Forman switched to outsourcing that work in just a couple of years. Yet the barrels being made for the core requirements of Jack Daniel’s remain unchanged.

As addressed in describing how Jack Daniel’s is produced, the barrels Lynchburg uses are made to a custom standard. Even the char level isn’t normal, falling between the standardized Level II and III. Neither Independent Stave Company nor any major cooperage in the US makes barrels like those used by Jack Daniel’s as one of their standardized products, which just underscores how that outsourcing is based on long-term contracts. Barrels generally are not normally bought off the shelf by even the smallest microdistillery, due to extremely high demand, but the scale and customized requirements makes that doubly the case for a Goliath like Jack Daniel’s.

All those barrels are made from white oaks, and for the most part, it takes 80 to 100 years to grow a tree mature enough for making staves. Some harvested trees are far older. Even among those mature enough to harvest, not every white oak in the forest is suitable for making barrel staves, and in no case is the entire tree used for this purpose. The most valuable parts could be used for making furniture, for example, while much of the tree could be junk grade, good only for firewood.

All other stages of barrel making can be ramped up in a matter of years. If more coopers, mill hands, or loggers are needed, those people can be hired and trained. When more output is required, the mills and cooperages can be built if the capital is there.

The one thing that can’t be done in the short- or middle term is increase the total stock of mature white oak in the forest. That can only be done over a lifetime or more, so the amount of wood available today is the result of choices, incidents, and accidents over the course of the last century.

Climate change poses a problem for the future supply of white oak. In my native Kentucky, the main concern with our area forests vis-à-vis white oak is how warmer temperatures are allowing other tree species to more aggressively colonize white oak ranges. The result would see beech, poplar, and red maple crowding out or crimping future white oak growth in wild forests.

Knowing this, Brown-Forman has paid close attention to forest sustainability. They first became concerned with the issue not over oak, but sugar maple. Starting in 1998, the company began cooperating with the University of Tennessee's School of Natural Resources to create seed orchards. Although these orchards include more tree species than just sugar maple and white oak, their purpose is to foster those two types of trees for whiskey production.

More recently, Brown-Forman is also heavily engaged with the nonprofit seed fund Dendrifund. That organization is partnered with the American Forest Foundation and the University of Kentucky in the White Oak Initiative, with the goal of regenerating 100 million acres of white oak forest by 2070. Dendrifund's board of directors is packed with Brown family members and Brown-Forman figures, including Chris Fletcher. When the Dendrifund website addresses water and watershed issues, a picture of Cave Spring is often there to underline the point.

The whiskey industry consumes about a tenth of the white oak harvested annually, and most estimates indicate that the forests can keep pace with demand for the next decade or two. After that, the predictions are that supplies will decline. The potential shortfall is partly a matter of increased demand, but also partly due to a sizable age gap in the forests. Most of the white oaks standing today are already mature or just entering maturity, and these grown oaks outnumber young trees by roughly three to one. That means there aren't many young trees coming up behind the stands of mature white oaks, and that is where having seed orchards and forest regeneration programs now will help close that age gap later in the century.

## Glass

After reaching the desired maturity—for Old No. 7, between four and five years of the average barrel—it's time to pull the barrel from the rickhouse, dump it, and collect the whiskey for batching. A whiskey like Old No. 7 uses a blend of barrel yields from separate floors and separate rickhouses to achieve the desired final product. The large volume of barrels dumped is essential because it marginalizes the impact of outlier barrels in the batch—those with peculiar flavors, most likely due to an eccentricity of the wood. This is a common practice in the world whiskey industry, as it helps achieve a consistent product from batch to batch while minimizing the labor-intensive handicraft of blending. At Jack Daniel's, a typical batch will draw on roughly 200 barrels, which is not especially large. Some major distillers will draw on several hundred barrels and casks per batch.

A footnote on the process of washing the used whiskey wood. You may have heard of this through the old distillery hand's tale of filling a freshly dumped bourbon barrel with several gallons of water, rolling that barrel down a hill, and coming out with several gallons of 35 proof bourbon for the hand to take home. At Jack Daniel's, it is not just the oak barrels that are soaked with whiskey; the sugar maple charcoal chips of the mellowing vats are as well. That might seem counterintuitive, since the point of that charcoal was to expensively remove unwanted compounds from the whiskey, but those compounds are stuck to the carbon in the charcoal. The whiskey can be washed from the wood without knocking undesirable elements loose. Both receive a wash of Cave Spring water, extracting whiskey from the wood, which is used in batching a variety of Jack Daniel's whiskey. The exact same process is what puts the hellfire into Jim Beam Devil's Cut.

With a batch of Old No. 7, Bonded Rye, or some other expression of Jack Daniel's, the final step is bottling. The bottling house isn't on the distillery tour, but truly curious visitors can still see it quite easily from the roadside—it lies in plain sight of the Fayetteville Highway. If you are driving to Fayetteville, the plant can be seen on the right side of the road (that drive will also take you past a small rickhouse complex on the left side of the road). This bottling plant sits on the same parcel as several more rickhouses and the Jack Daniel's Firehouse. Inside this cavernous building, the bottles are filled, labeled, boxed, and shipped off to bars, liquor stores, and restaurants around the globe.

JACK DANIEL'S
Old No.7 BRAND
Tennessee
SOUR MASH
WHISKEY
1.75 Litre 40% Vol.
QUALITY & CRAFTSMANSHIP SINCE 1866

JACK DANIEL'S
Old
No.7
BRAND
Tennessee
SOUR MASH
WHISKEY
1.75 Litre 40% Vol.

In case Emergency Dial 3111
JUNE 2024
Acknowledge
[Capper] Line Stopped
GENTLEMAN JACK

B2 – Inspection Work Station
GENTLEMAN JACK

JACK DANIEL'S
CINNAMON SPICE
Tennessee
FIRE
FINELY CRAFTED
CINNAMON LIQUEUR
FROM THE MAKERS OF JACK DANIEL'S
TENNESSEE WHISKEY
70cl e 35% Vol.
JACK DANIEL DISTILLERY
QUALITY & CRAFTSMANSHIP
JACK DANIEL'S
Old No.7 BRAND
Tennessee
SOUR MASH
WHISKEY
70cl 40% Vol.
DISTILLED AND BOTTLED BY
JACK DANIEL DISTILLERY
LYNCHBURG, TENNESSEE 37352 U.S.A.
EVERY DROP MADE IN LYNCHBURG TENNESSEE
QUALITY & CRAFTSMANSHIP SINCE 1866
Old No.7 BRAND
JACK DANIEL DISTILLERY
ORIGINAL RECIPE
Tennessee
HONEY
FINELY CRAFTED
HONEY LIQUEUR
FROM THE MAKERS OF JACK DANIEL'S
TENNESSEE WHISKEY
70cl 35% Vol. e

# Expressions

Old
No.7
BRAND
JACK DANIEL'S
Old
No.7
BRAND
Tennessee
SOUR MASH
WHISKEY
DISTILLED & BOTTLED BY
JACK DANIEL DISTILLERY
LYNCHBURG, TENN. USA
40% ALC BY VOL. (80 PROOF)
EVERY DROP MADE IN LYNCHBURG TENNESSEE
QUALITY & CRAFTSMANSHIP SINCE 1866

## Jack Daniel's Old No. 7

Jack Daniel's Old No. 7 Tennessee Whiskey is ubiquitous and consequently goes by many informal names, such as JD, Black Label, and simply "Jack." This is the classic expression with a brand identity and distribution reach rivaling its mixer-mate Coca-Cola.

Most of what Jack Daniel's does is a derivative of Old No. 7—some older, some stronger, others more selectively or restrictively selected/batched or given a round of secondary maturation. That is nothing to scoff at. When you look at the lineup of any major distillery, that list is composed of many separately named variations on just a handful of stock whiskeys. At least in this line, all the tweaks on Old No. 7 still bear the name Jack Daniel's, so in that respect the line as a whole is rather transparent.

As described in the production chapter, Old No. 7 is made from a mash of 80 percent corn, 8 percent rye, and 12 percent malted barley. Compared to Kentucky bourbons, the mash bill is high corn and very low rye. From there, the process should be very familiar with whiskey fans with two major exceptions: drip filtration through sugar maple charcoal and the choice of standard barrel stock used by Jack Daniel's. Although all Tennessee Whiskeys must be charcoal mellowed prior to barreling, the method used in Lynchburg is (thus far) unique to Jack Daniel's. Likewise, their combination of long toasting and short charring for their barrels is idiosyncratic.

Although it has been Jack Daniel's flagship whiskey for decades and is built on a foundation of traditional methods, Old No. 7 has not gone unchanged over the years. In 1987, the decision was made to cut the strength to 86 proof. The whiskey was cut again in 2004, to 80 proof.

The nose on Old No. 7 combines a very bourbon-y stream of vanilla and caramel with Lynchburg's trademark banana note, plus a little nuttiness and a hint of spice. The latter pair provides just enough of a contrast to help balance out what is otherwise a sweet and tropical fruity scent. The palate holds onto and develops that character. The sweet side adds some candy corn to the caramel, banana, and vanilla; the nuttiness goes from nondescript to slightly pecan and peanut; the spiciness leans into cinnamon. The finish runs with the sweet elements and a little oak tannin, lingering on that last note as it fades. Above all, this is a supremely mellow whiskey, especially compared to its peers. A testament to how much preconceived notions shape perception, my take on Old No. 7 and its virtues has changed, and part of that had to do with the years when I lived overseas, where JD was the only American whiskey I could reliably get. My appreciation for this staple expression thus grew over time.

JACK

## Gentleman Jack

Any discussion of Gentleman Jack should start with what American whiskey as a whole was at the time of its release in 1988. The first side of that is inside Jack Daniel's itself. The year before, Old No. 7 was cut from 90 to 86 proof, and of the company's two other regular expressions, one was down market from the core Jack Daniel's Black Label, Lem Motlow Sour Mash. The other, Jack Daniel's Green Label, was intended as an even easier-drinking spin on Old No. 7.

The other side is that the mid- and late 1980s were when premium American whiskey was embryonic. Maker's Mark was coming into its own that decade, while Elijah Craig and Blanton's were newcomers. Van Winkle bourbons were still being sourced out of Stitzel-Weller Distillery, bottled in Lawrenceburg, Kentucky, and relatively obscure. Most of the big names in premium whiskey either had not yet been created or were moribund, waiting for the twenty-first century for recycling and revival.

Premium whiskey as we think of it today was barely a thing when Gentleman Jack came out, and for this expression Jack Daniel's decided to double down on what it was known for: charcoal mellowing and the consequent smoothness. All Jack Daniel's whiskeys receive a round of charcoal mellowing before barreling, but Gentleman Jack receives a second round after barrel dumping. This is essentially tacking onto the existing Old No. 7 process what Jim Beam did with its Green Label and Ezra Brooks still does today.

The whiskey was also bottled at 80 proof. Nowadays, regular Old No. 7 is, as well, but recall that was not the case when Gentleman Jack was introduced, and Old No. 7 would remain a stronger whiskey for a decade and a half afterward. I revisited Gentleman Jack in preparing this book, and what I found was a whiskey that leads with a nose of simple fruity sweetness, like syrup from a can of fruit salad plus fresh bananas, married to a dollop of caramel. Behind that was a hint of oak and spice. On the palate, the fruitiness gets trimmed down to just the bananas, with the sweet aspect moving more over to a bourbonized brown sugar and honey. The finish is smooth, clean, and only marginally woody.

If the point was to double down on smoothness and approachability, Gentleman Jack hit the bull's-eye. When taken side by side, I find its structure better defined than Old No. 7, but without becoming complex or intense. It is so easy drinking without losing character that I wish Gentleman Jack, rather than Old No. 7, was the gateway whiskey for so many young people out there.

JACK DANIEL'S
GENTLEMAN
JACK
DOUBLE MELLOWED • TENNESSEE WHISKEY
40% VOL
DISTILLED & BOTTLED BY
JACK DANIEL DISTILLERY
LYNCHBURG, TN. USA
70cL

JACK DANIEL'S
GENTLEMAN
JACK
DOUBLE MELLOWED • TENNESSEE WHISKEY
Jack Daniel
40% VOL
DISTILLED & BOTTLED BY
JACK DANIEL DISTILLERY
LYNCHBURG, TN. USA
70cL

"Gentleman Jack hit the bull's-eye. When taken side by side, I find its structure better defined than Old No. 7, but without becoming complex or intense. It is so easy drinking without losing character that I wish Gentleman Jack, rather than Old No. 7, was the gateway whiskey for so many young people out there."

# Jack Daniel's Bonded

The Bottled in Bond Act of 1897 was a measure of the reformist Progressive Era, part of a wave of measures intended to ensure the quality of drink, food, and medicine. It preceded Upton Sinclair's famous novel *The Jungle* by seven years, making it one of the earliest legislative achievements of the era, due in larger part to the support of many of the key bourbon distillers of the age. Jack Daniel himself played no part in its passage—in keeping with his disdain for politics. George Garvin Brown, founder of the company that became Brown-Forman, was an opponent, since he was a non-distiller producer (NDP), and the measure favored products made by actual distillers.

The law grants the designation of "Bottled in Bond" to whiskeys that come from a single distillery, are at least four years old, come from the stock made in a single distilling season, and are bottled at 100 proof. An additional provision that the whiskey be aged in a government-supervised warehouse mattered quite a bit in the days when tax officials were a regular presence at distilleries, but less so today, although it remains on the books.

Bonded whiskeys have enjoyed something of a comeback in recent years, leading to the appearance Jack Daniel's Bottled in Bond in 2018. This was a travel retail–only expression (i.e., only available in airport duty-free shops) coming in one-liter bottles. Four years later, the company chose to repackage this bonded version of Old No. 7 as Jack Daniel's Bonded, releasing it in tandem with Jack Daniel's Triple Mash Bonded to kick off their new Bonded series.

The Bonded series has a catch, though—the standard size for the bottling is the internationalized 700 ml, rather than the 750-ml American fifth bottle. The US government dropped its insistence on the 750-ml standard at the end of 2020, paving the way for some companies to simplify their logistics by putting some of their expressions in the smaller bottles and shipping them anywhere and everywhere. Some critics cite it as an example of shrinkflation. For my part, I prefer the classic fifth bottle, but I'm not going to join an impassioned social media crusade over what is literally one extra shot of whiskey.

A pour of Jack Daniel's Bonded has a classical mid-amber coloring. The scent is just as classic: brown sugar and caramel sweet, a touch spicy, a touch nutty, plus a bit of char. The mellowness comes through in how it does not feel any stronger than the standard Old No. 7, despite the extra 20 points in proof. The flavor profile keeps the brown sugar, caramel, and nuttiness, but to this adds a little creamy banana milkshake. The finish turns a bit spicy and a bit woody and lingers for a spell. Those bonded tweaks to Jack Daniel's take the core flavor profile of Old No. 7 and build on it, rather than carrying it off to different places.

Jack Daniel
100
PROOF
JACK DANIEL'S
BONDED
TENNESSEE WHISKEY
AGED IN SELECT BARRELS FOR
ADDED DEPTH AND CHARACTER
BOTTLED-IN-BOND · 100 PROOF
50% ALC./VOL. 700mL

JACK DANIEL
DISTILLERY
DSP-TN-1
TENNESSEE

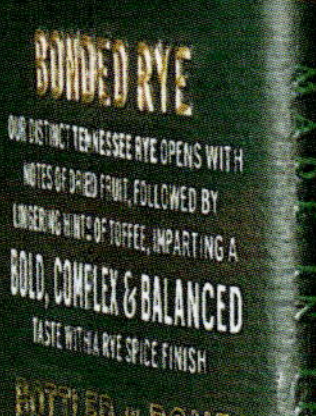
Jack Daniel's
100
PROOF
BONDED RYE
BOLD, COMPLEX & BALANCED
BOTTLED-IN-BOND
100 PROOF
JACK DANIEL'S
BONDED RYE
TENNESSEE RYE WHISKEY
UNIQUELY CRAFTED RYE GRAIN BILL
DELIVERS A BOLD AND COMPLEX FLAVOR
BOTTLED-IN-BOND · 100 PROOF
50% ALC./VOL. 700mL
JACK DANIEL
DISTILLERY
DSP-TN-1
TENNESSEE

## Jack Daniel's Bonded Rye

The revamped Jack Daniel's Bonded and the Bonded Triple Mash were critical hits in 2022, which prompted the company to look for a way to expand the series. Eyes soon settled on their rye whiskey. So, 11 years into making rye whiskey with the Lynchburg style, Jack Daniel's raised the bar on their standard version and created Jack Daniel's Bonded Rye.

The mash recipe behind JD rye was almost the complete opposite of the distillery's house Tennessee Whiskey recipe, which is noted for being very heavy on the corn (80 percent) and light on the rye (8 percent). Their rye, on the other hand, is 70 percent rye, 18 percent corn, and 12 percent malted barley. Compared to its predecessor—Jack Daniel's Straight Rye—the bonded version is 10 points stronger (100 proof), a little more expensive, and (unofficially) a few years older. Although it bears no age statement, the word from the company at the time of launch was that Bonded Rye came from the Spring 2016 distilling season, making it seven years old when it was prepared for the market. That may fluctuate over time, but they will keep the flavor profile consistent. Furthermore, I expect this expression to stay at least a year or two older than the Straight Rye ever was, and thus a whole step above the minimum four-year age of a bonded whiskey. Against that, it is part of the Jack Daniel's Bonded series, so it comes in two internationalized sizes, 700 ml and one liter.

Pours of the Bonded Rye have that lighter copper coloring so characteristic of rye whiskeys. The scent presents itself as a fruit salad of pear, tangerine, and banana with a drizzle of molasses and vanilla, coupled with notes of herbal seasonings and evergreen. Those spices grew bolder on the palate, turning to a dash of cinnamon, a pinch of black pepper, and a clutch of mint sprigs and pine needles. The sweet fruit took a step back while remaining at center stage, a transition that brought the whiskey into better balance. Throw in a little barrel char, and you've got the whole thing. The finish ran with the barrel char and pepper notes but was a light touch, and neither element lingered.

When it was released in late 2023, Jack Daniel's Bonded Rye was slated to replace the Straight Rye version. Although a little more expensive and coming in a somewhat smaller bottle, the Bonded Rye still offers plenty of bang for the buck. As I write this, both the Bonded and Straight bottlings are still readily available on store shelves, making a side-by-side comparison easy.

# Jack Daniel's Bonded Triple Mash

At the same time Jack Daniel's Bottled in Bond was revamped into Jack Daniel's Bonded, they also took the three separate whiskeys then in production and blended them into a hybrid to create Jack Daniel's Bonded Triple Mash. That blend drew on the Tennessee Whiskey behind Old No. 7 for 20 percent, the new rye whiskey stock for 60 percent, and the even newer single malt whiskey for the last 20 percent. Prior to Triple Mash, Jack Daniel's had only offered their malt whiskey as a one-time special release, and since American Single Malt would not come out until 2023, this was actually the first expression in regular release to utilize their latest malt whiskey mash bill.

As a bonded whiskey, all three constituent whiskeys must comply with the guidelines set out by the Bottled in Bond Act of 1897. The whiskeys are all at least four years old and made at Jack Daniel's. Each of the lots of whiskey selected for use in a batch of Triple Mash must have been made in a single distilling season. As a Jack Daniel's product, all three received charcoal mellowing, as everything does at the distillery. Finally, after batching and cutting, the whiskey is bottled at 100 proof.

Some folks try to pull the individual elements out of the Triple Mash, which is an interesting exercise. Jack Daniel's American Single Malt has an oloroso sherry cask finish, as did the Twice Barreled expression before it. So, if you can separate the Tennessee Whiskey and the rye from the hybrid in your imagination, this is your best crack at getting to what the not-finished Jack Daniel's malt is like.

The aroma comes across as oatmeal cookie dough with an extra-heavy helping of baking spices (cinnamon, ginger, and nutmeg) stirred in. On the palate, the whiskey has the trademark Jack Daniel's mellowness, but with a weightier mouthfeel than customary. The flavor turns from cookies to banana bread, albeit one with plenty of the aforementioned cookie spice blend and some vanilla added. My opinion is the malt whiskey part of the hybrid presents itself more with the heaviness of the pour than in its taste, as malts tend to be weightier. The finish delivers a soft current of spiciness.

Jack Daniel's
100
PROOF
JACK DANIEL'S
TRIPLE MASH®
BLENDED STRAIGHT WHISKEY
A BLEND OF BONDED AMERICAN MALT,
RYE, AND TENNESSEE WHISKEYS
BOTTLED-IN-BOND · 100 PROOF
50% ALC./VOL. 700mL
MADE IN TENNESSEE
BOTTLED AT THE DISTILLERY

JACK DANIEL
DISTILLERY
DSP-TN-1
TENNESSEE

SELECT
JACK DANIEL'S
UNIQUELY CRAFTED
HANDMADE BARRELS
SINGLE BARREL
SELECT
TENNESSEE WHISKEY
47% ALC/VOL 750ML
LYNCHBURG
TENN.
MASTER DISTILLED

## Jack Daniel's Single Barrel Select

Back when Jack Daniel was learning the ropes of the whiskey business, if you got your whiskey from a reputable grocer or saloon, it was probably all single barrel. If you bought a stoneware jug of Jack Daniel's instead, it was probably also single barrel. If not, it would have had whiskey from two barrels in it at most—the end of the last barrel and the start of the next one. That was the nature of the business back then, because affordable, mass-produced glass bottles only came later in Daniel's career. But with that industrial process came the idea of mass batching barrels of whiskey to achieve a consistent bottled product.

So one way of looking at the 1997 introduction of the 94-proof Jack Daniel's Single Barrel is as a return to Daniel's late nineteenth–century way of doing things. The first single barrel bourbon was Blanton's, made in 1984 by what would eventually become Buffalo Trace Distillery, following in the footsteps of the marketing success that single malt Scotch whiskys were enjoying at the time. The idea was to select barrels of particular merit and bottle a batch straight from them. The nearest equivalent to that original JD Single Barrel release nowadays is the modern Single Barrel Select at 90 proof.

Jack Daniel's Tennessee Whiskey is, by definition, not supposed to be ballsy, and Single Barrel Select is no exception. As a single barrel whiskey, it also displays variability from barrel to barrel. Usually this is small, perhaps so small you would only notice it in a guided tasting of examples, but sometimes it can be quite marked. The latter is what private barrel offerings emphasize, so if your Jack Daniel's Single Barrel Select is offered as just from that store or bar, expect a different experience.

In the glass, the whiskey has a darkened copper look to it, while the aroma displays a sweet character from its notes of candy corn, banana chips, and vanilla, accented by toasted oak and a hint of nuts. Sipping on the whiskey has the Jack Daniel's signature of a mellow experience, and it is quite sweet, with brown sugar and vanilla, plus slices of fresh banana. A few slivers of spicy, minty, oak-driven flavor have just enough presence to keep things interesting, but without disturbing its relaxing nature.

Jack Daniel
JACK DANIEL'S
UNIQUELY CRAFTED
HANDMADE BARRELS
SINGLE BARREL
SELECT
TENNESSEE WHISKEY
70cl 45% Vol.
LYNCHBURG
TENN.
MASTER DISTILLED

HANDMADE BARRELS
LYNCHBURG
TENN.

100 PROOF
Jack Daniel
JACK DANIEL'S
UNIQUELY CRAFTED
HANDMADE BARRELS
SINGLE BARREL
100 PROOF
TENNESSEE WHISKEY
50% ALC/VOL 750ML
LYNCHBURG
TENN.
BOTTLED IN BOND

## Jack Daniel's Single Barrel 100 Proof

Concurrent with the introduction of the original 94 proof Jack Daniel's Single Barrel was another version of their Tennessee Whiskey done as a single barrel, Jack Daniel's Silver Select. This version relied on barrels that were even more specially chosen than the regular Jack Daniel's Single Barrel and was bottled at the higher strength of 100 proof to boot. It was, however, largely unknown to Americans, as it was available only in certain foreign markets and in airport duty-free shops.

Jack Daniel's Silver Select was essentially revamped into the Single Barrel 100 Proof Bottled in Bond in 2016, and while they were at it, Brown-Forman brought the expression home ... kind of. Bottles still bear the label "Traveler's Exclusive" on the back, and technically are still meant for foreign markets and duty-free shops, but one can get them in the US from select retailers. This version of Jack Daniel's is colloquially referred to as "Single Barrel 100 Proof" because the Bottled in Bond part on the label is so small as to be a footnote. It is clearly intended to be third in prominence among the whiskey's indicated characteristics. Also, the two designations—single barrel and bottled in bond—are not mutually exclusive. The former requires that all the whiskey come from just one barrel, and there is nothing in the requirements of the Bottled in Bond Act of 1897 that precludes drawing from just a single barrel for bottling.

When I first tried the two in the early 2000s, I thought Silver Select was markedly better than the Jack Daniel's Single Barrel. Nowadays, I think they are much more on the same level, and the differences can be chalked up to single barrel variance and how the extra 5 percent alcohol changes flavor perception.

The look of a pour is light amber, and while the nose is just as sweet as Single Barrel Select, it's a touch oily. The candy corn and vanilla are still the backbone of the aroma, but the banana note requires a bit of time to develop, while the nutty and woody elements are more in evidence. That introduction is indicative of what comes next. Although still sweet and mellow in the main, at 100 proof the liquid is a little drier and woodier. The finish winds down as a statement on that drift—mellow, but with the oak stepping up enough to bring the drink into much better balance than the Single Barrel Select.

## Jack Daniel's Single Barrel Barrel Proof

Perhaps the only way to get closer to the essence of the original Jack Daniel's whiskey than a single barrel offering is a single barrel at cask strength. Back then, if whiskey was served at the saloon, more often than not that would be from single barrel, but with water added (complaints about barkeeps watering down drinks are as old as recorded history). Surviving examples of the old stoneware Jack Daniel's jugs from the pre-bottle decades don't have *proof* printed on them, so it is unclear if those were cut with water or not. Taking your own bottle to the grocer, as was the practice until the end of the nineteenth century, ensured you could pay for the undiluted stuff, straight from the barrel.

Barrel proof means exactly that: at the strength the whiskey held when the barrel was dumped, no water added. Because the angel's share is different for every barrel, even when those two barrels sit right next to each other in the rickhouse, bottling at cask strength adds to the variability already found in single barrel expressions. My notebook says I have tried Jack Daniel's Single Barrel Barrel Proof whiskeys that came out at 130.9 proof, 130.6 proof, 128.7 proof, and 128.2 proof. Those were all potent pours, and each one had a common core (which I will address), but also its own distinct qualities (which I will not).

Introduced in 2015, Jack Daniel's Single Barrel Barrel Proof was a whiskey that changed more than a few minds among whiskey bloggers, many of whom said they were giving Jack a fresh look after trying it. That included the contributor who wrote about a 2016 bottling for my own website, *The Whiskey Reviewer*.

As one might expect from uncut whiskey, these always come out dark, the amber coloring leaning heavily into brown. The liquid is often so viscous that it takes a couple of minutes for legs to appear after swirling the glass. I have never found Jack Daniel's whiskeys ballsy, but this one is certainly bold and full. The candy corn, brown sugar, vanilla, and banana chips come right up out of the glass to shake hands, and that grip is firm. Caramel, sweet corn, and brown sugar coat the mouth on a sip, almost like syrup. And that is what you get even after adding some water, as I often do with pours that rise above 120 proof.

BARREL
PROOF
Jack Daniel
JACK DANIEL'S
UNIQUELY CRAFTED
HANDMADE BARRELS
SINGLE BARREL
BARREL PROOF
TENNESSEE WHISKEY
LYNCHBURG
TENN.
MASTER DISTILLED
SELECT
130.9 PROOF | 65% ALC/VOL | 750ML

## Jack Daniel's Single Barrel Rye

For the latter half of the twentieth century and well into the twenty-first, Jack Daniel's had something in common with both their neighbors at George Dickel and Maker's Mark in Kentucky: they were the only big distillers in the business of making just the one thing. These three each had one yeast, one mash bill, and made one kind of whiskey. Even if Daniel's had Gentleman Jack and Jack Daniel's Single Barrel back in the day, those were all based off the same distillate as Old No. 7.

That changed in 2012. Dickel, for one, outsourced some rye whiskey from MGP of Indiana, the old Seagram's distillery that has become the prime supplier of ready-aged whiskey for NDPs in America. Jack Daniel's also sought to enter the thriving rye whiskey game that year, but they took the long route and made it themselves. They developed their first new mash bill in a century, 70 percent rye, 18 percent corn, and 12 percent malted barley, flipping the script on the high-corn, low-rye approach embodied in the traditional Daniel's mash bill. Some 26 members of the distillery team participated in developing the new rye whiskey.

Fixing upon that mash led immediately to the release of an unaged ("white") rye in 2012. Even though this white rye wasn't matured, it still saw the same Lincoln County Process after distillation that all whiskeys made in Lynchburg receive. This bottling was followed by a minimally aged two-year-old rye in 2014, the Jack Daniel's Rested Tennessee Rye, as a preview of what was to come. Both the precursors were limited-edition releases, discontinued for years now. The first Jack Daniel's rye to enter regular release and stay with us was the Single Barrel Rye, which came out in 2016. That also grew their Single Barrel Collection to three expressions (Select, Barrel Proof, and now Rye). In a departure from what virtually every other whiskey company in America was doing, Jack Daniel's chose to bottle this one with a maroon label, rather than the usual "green for rye" label.

Bottled at 94 proof, the Single Barrel Rye I sat down with came across with only a modest note of rye spice on the nose, compared to the heftier scents of vanilla, red berries, and banana. As a sipper, the whiskey has an oily mouthfeel, and leads with the same vanilla, red berries, and now fried banana. The cookie spices and a sliver of oak sit behind that but rise on the back end and come to dominate in the finish. It's mostly cinnamon and dry oak lingering on afterward, but the initial hint of vanilla adds some dimension to that conclusion. Again, this is a single barrel, so expect some variance from bottling to bottling.

RYE
JACK DANIEL'S
UNIQUELY CRAFTED
HANDMADE BARRELS
SINGLE BARREL
RYE
TENNESSEE RYE WHISKEY
47% ALC/ VOL 750ML
LYNCHBURG
TENN.
MASTER DISTILLED

## Jack Daniel's Single Barrel Barrel Proof Rye

The romantic charms of getting whiskey straight from the barrel, uncut, are popular with enthusiasts and casual drinkers alike. Whiskeys over 120 proof are probably best enjoyed with some water added, though, which is why cask-strength bottlings are best seen as concentrates. When straight from the barrel is too hot to be fully enjoyed, one can add water and dial that down to suit individual taste.

As part of their expanded Single Barrel line, Jack Daniel's added this Barrel Proof version of the Single Barrel Rye, at first as a special release and then as a permanent brand extension. Examples are expected to range from 125 to 145 proof, so all will be very strong, with some crossing the 140 mark and entering into the "Hazmat" category of ultra-strong whiskeys.

My samplings of the Single Barrel Barrel Proof Rye made me think of a rye cookie. The aroma leads with baking spices, a hint of cooked porridge, and dried flower petals. On the palate, that porridge/cooked wheat/hot oatmeal aspect takes a step forward, giving the whiskey more balance. The flowery note from the nose turns into a peppermint strand, and the flavor profile picks up a nutty note. The finish goes down spicy and a touch dry.

## Jack Daniel's American Single Malt

The American Single Malt has been the "next big thing" in American whiskey since the middle 2010s, steadily gaining momentum as a category while never quite arriving. For much of that time, it was the province of craft and mid-sized distillers, who were engaged in the wise business practice of moving into those territories where the big distillers were not. As the movement grew, those big distillers began paying attention. However, Jack Daniel's had actually been planning to introduce a single malt since at least 2015. Those designs led to a development pattern not dissimilar to how the distillery introduced their rye: first a youthful, one-time limited edition single malt release, then the single malt was used in the Jack Daniel's Triple Mash hybrid whiskey, and now, finally, in a proper Jack Daniel's single malt whiskey.

American single malts share most characteristics in common with single malt whiskey as it is understood in Scotland, Japan, Ireland, and elsewhere. The grain used is 100 percent malted barley, the whiskey comes from a single distillery, and the casks used to age do not need to be new (although they certainly can be). The major distinction for most American distillers is that whereas the rest of the world mandates that malt whiskey be made in pot stills, this is not required in the United States. Jack Daniel's only has column

“The American Single Malt has been the ‘next big thing’ in American whiskey since the middle 2010s.”

stills, and but a handful of the distillers making American single malts have a set of true pot stills.

To this, add the mandatory Jack Daniel’s step of the Lincoln County Process. After charcoal mellowing, the single malt distillate is entered into new white oak barrels for five years, then finished in 79.25-gallon sherry casks for a further three years. After eight years of total aging, this Tennessee-meets-Scotland whiskey was bottled at 90 proof.

In the glass, the whiskey looks like strong black tea with red highlights. A nosing of this thick, potent whiskey leads with boozy four-berry jam, strongly underscoring the sherry cask finish. Behind that sherry influence is buckwheat honey and vanilla. Sipping on the malt reveals the boozy berry current from the nose joined by earthy cocoa, again laid over vanilla and dark buckwheat honey. Finally, the finish turns to raisins and toasted oat bread smeared with honey before turning lightly peppered. Strangely absent, at least to my palate, was Jack’s characteristic banana note.

This is an intensely flavorful whiskey, but one that is quite outside the familiar Jack Daniel’s wheelhouse, even more so than the Tennessee Rye. That said, it certainly occupies the midpoint between Tennessee Whiskey and Scotch whisky, and those who like a good pour of Speyside malt will recognize it as astride the path to a sherry bomb. Finally, like everything coming out of Lynchburg, it is supremely smooth, and this despite its potent flavors.

# Jack Daniel's 10 Year Old

Although Jack Daniel's joined the game of having more than one mash bill in production and a double-digit number of expressions available for regular release in the middle 2010s, the company remained stubborn on the issue of age statements. It's not that Jack Daniel's whiskeys have never borne an age statement, but the last time that was the case was before Prohibition. During the Bourbon Boom, when ultra-aged bourbons and rye whiskeys garnered particular attention right and left, the lack of an age statement adorning any Jack Daniel's label was curious to some and a major misfire to others. Mind you, some of those high age-statement bourbons were definitely over-oaked, whereas Mr. Jack's whiskey continued to underscore its mellowness, but the void was noticed all the same. Of Jack Daniel's two rivals for global sales supremacy and reach, Jim Beam often puts age statements on its whiskeys, and Johnnie Walker regularly does. Jack Daniel's may or may not have actually come late to the modern practice of having a large range of expressions on the market, but the brand inarguably came late to age statements.

It ultimately fell to Chris Fletcher and Lexie Phillips to introduce the first regular release age-statement Jack Daniel's anyone living can remember, and they did so in 2021. More goes into this older take on Old No. 7 than one might expect because it is aged on the top of a given rickhouse for seven or eight of those years before being moved down to the bottom floor. The upper reaches of a rickhouse are sweltering in summer, which speeds up the chemical transformations taking place in the whiskey. However, it also increases evaporation and the absorption of flavors from the wood, so shifting the barrel to the always cooler, damper ground floor puts the brakes on the process during the latter stages. Moving barrels is an unusual extra step in the maturation process, and one not typically associated with Jack Daniel's.

The expression was invented as one coming out in discrete annual batches, so it occupies shelf space behind store counters or in locked display cabinets—and shouldn't be expected there year-round.

Starting right with the nose, you can identify it as part of the Old No. 7 family—though it stands out as so much more than just Old No. 7. With a scent led by brown sugar, caramel, and fried plantains, the nose is enhanced by the spiciness of cinnamon, peppermint, and oak. Once on the palate, a pour of this whiskey becomes noticeably drier compared to the predictably mellow Jack Daniel's standard, developing much more character along the way. The sweet side deepens with notes of a mix of dark dried fruits, like raisins and cherries, but the dry spices and oak are more present than on the nose as well, so the sweet and spicy sides stay in balance. The finish rolls on with the oaky spices, adding a leathery character into the mix.

JACK DANIEL'S
10
YEARS OLD
TENNESSEE WHISKEY
DISTILLED AND BOTTLED BY
JACK DANIEL DISTILLERY
LYNCHBURG, TENNESSEE, USA
EST. & REG. IN 1866
48.5% ALC./VOL. 97 PROOF | BATCH 02

A 10 year old is almost pushing the top of what I would call merely "mature" for American whiskeys; I don't start labeling a whiskey middle-aged until it reaches 12 years old. Even so, the extra barrel time makes a clear showing here. The expression, which is bottled at 97 proof, won high marks from experts and persuaded some more of the bourbon enthusiast holdouts who had been stubbornly refusing to give Jack Daniel's a second look the motivation to finally relent.

## Jack Daniel's 12 Year Old

Following the release of the 10 Year Old was the Jack Daniel's 12 Year Old, the first batch of which was put out in 2023. An interesting footnote in the development of Jack Daniel's age-statement whiskeys is that Chris Fletcher came on board as Jeff Arnett's deputy in January 2014. He may not have been there when the initial 10 Year Old and 12 Year Old barrels were filled, but he was certainly there far enough back to have been enmeshed in developing the barrel selection process for what goes into these whiskeys from square one.

That development and selection matters, because even though this is the same distillate as Old No. 7 and only a notional two years older than its precursor, the 12 Year Old is a very different creature. For one thing, it is bottled at a whopping 107 proof, 10 points higher than the 10 Year Old and 27 beyond the standard Black Label. I like to think both the age and the strength are shouting at the drinker right from the pour, what with the dark, deep red, amber coloring of the liquid.

The nose comes across as a hunk of banana topped with dried cherries and caked in caramel, plus a note of butterscotch. Imagine an ice cream sundae, but without the ice cream. In the main, it's a very sweet scent, but one with a decidedly musty current running through it. It's that latter part, the mustiness, that gives the aroma some serious character.

With the sip, the flavor profile continueds with the fruity sweetness from the nose, along with notes of maple and vanilla. From there it turns a touch spicy and woody, a turn that again endows the whiskey with more character than mere sweetness can provide. The finish rolls off that latter point in part, being leathery and tannic on one hand, but also a little like rum raisin on the other.

Chris Fletcher has said the distillery has intentions to introduce even older expressions in the future, which proved true with the 2025 arrival of Jack Daniel's. Fletcher has suggested the line will go as far as 21. That would certainly be making up for lost time, landing in the same territory as some of the oldest whiskeys introduced by Heaven Hill and Pappy Van Winkle.

JACK DANIEL'S
12
YEARS OLD
TENNESSEE WHISKEY
DISTILLED AND BOTTLED BY
JACK DANIEL DISTILLERY
LYNCHBURG, TENNESSEE, USA
EST. & REG. IN 1866
53.5% ALC./VOL. 107 PROOF | BATCH 01

JACK DANIEL'S
12
YEARS OLD
TENNESSEE WHISKEY
DISTILLED AND BOTTLED BY
JACK DANIEL DISTILLERY
LYNCHBURG, TENNESSEE, USA
EST. & REG. IN 1866
53.5 % ALC./VOL. 107 PROOF | BATCH 02
JACK DANIEL'S
10
YEARS OLD
TENNESSEE WHISKEY
DISTILLED AND BOTTLED BY
JACK DANIEL DISTILLERY
LYNCHBURG, TENNESSEE, USA
EST. & REG. IN 1866
48.5 % ALC./VOL. 97 PROOF | BATCH 03

JACK DANIEL'S
10
YEARS OLD
TENNESSEE WHISKEY
DISTILLED AND BOTTLED BY
JACK DANIEL DISTILLERY
LYNCHBURG, TENNESSEE, USA
EST. & REG. IN 1866
97 PROOF | BATCH 02
LIMITED RELEASE
JACK DANIEL'S
12
YEARS OLD
TENNESSEE WHISKEY
DISTILLED AND BOTTLED BY
JACK DANIEL DISTILLERY
LYNCHBURG, TENNESSEE, USA
EST. & REG. IN 1866
53.5% ALC./VOL. 107 PROOF | BATCH 01

## Jack Daniel's 14 Year Old

Most recent in the Jack Daniel's age-statement series was the 2025 unveiling of their 14 Year Old, and it was quite a departure from the preceding installments. The 10 and 12 Year Olds were strong whiskeys, but the 14 Year Old is cask strength, with the 2025 batch coming in at a whopping 126.3 proof. Despite this, it remains supremely mellow, showing no hint of its potency on nosing or sipping. I routinely add water to whiskeys over 120 proof, but I found this one didn't really require it, although some may argue it would still be improved by a few drops.

The nose leads with dried cherries, syrupy brown sugar, and a roll of nuttiness and woodiness. Further nosing brings out a hoary leather note plus a light hint of banana—this latter note, so customary to Jack, lying half-buried by all the other scent elements. In terms of flavor, the syrupy character suggested by the nosing finds its expression as a viscous mouthfeel. It is a thick liquid, with a hefty helping of chocolate- and caramel-covered dried cherries and raspberries, with just one banana chip that feels like it somehow found its way in by accident. Coming on behind that are notes of cinnamon and dry oak. The finish rolls over on to a pleasant oaky note, before fading down to leave behind a long lasting trace of nuts, so the finish makes a callback to that conjoined woody-nutty aspect from the nose.

## Jack Daniel's Distillery Series/Tennessee Tasters

A regular feature for many big distillers is the experimental series, which sees the use of a speculative mash bill, unorthodox choice of finishing cask, extra-long fermentation time, exotic yeast, or some other twist on that distiller's whiskey-making process. Jack Daniel's is no exception, having started a series called Tennessee Tasters back in 2018, and making it available only at the distillery and with a few select retailers in Tennessee (so, a de facto distillery-only release). Released in 375-ml, flask-style bottles with plain white labeling, the look of the Tennessee Tasters whiskeys is reminiscent of the sample bottles used in the lab by evaluation panels. In 2022, the line was renamed the Distillery Series but remains unchanged in terms of bottling or appearance.

The inaugural release for the series was High Angel's Share, which came from a lot of five-year-old Tennessee Whiskey barrels that saw unusually high evaporation. That release was done at 107 proof, but as a rule the expressions of the series are 100 proof and focus on unusual cask choices for a round of finishing. Yet sometimes they revert to the High Angel's Share model, featuring stronger whiskey and focusing on an aspect like barrels drawn from a particular spot in one rickhouse, such as the 2019 Barrel Proof Rye. Examples

DSP
TN-1
JACK DANIEL'S
DISTILLERY SERIES
TWICE BARRELED
TENNESSEE STRAIGHT RYE WHISKEY
DSP-TN-1
A unique rye grain bill twice barreled in new, charred American white oak barrels for added depth and character.
LIMITED EDITION
PROOF 107 | ALC/VOL 53.5% | SIZE 375ml
SELECTION # 013 | RELEASED July 2024
SELECTED BY WHISKEY TASTER, JASON MARSKI

of some of the stranger barrel choices for the Distillery Series have been using maple (Jeff Arnett has said the maple barrels were particularly problematic, being fragile and leaky), Jamaican allspice wood, pecan wood, charred hickory staves inserted into the barrels, or used añejo tequila barrels.

I have sampled half of the releases in this series and have always found them interesting tweaks on their base expressions. Some, however, have exceeded that baseline and stood out as excellent, like the Barrel Proof Rye. For most Jack Daniel's fans, coming across one will prove difficult, as they are generally unavailable outside of the Volunteer State. That makes snagging one at the distillery's White Rabbit bottle shop a must-do agenda item during a visit.

## Jack Daniel's Single Barrel Heritage Barrel

One of the Jack Daniel's Single Barrel whiskeys stands separate from the rest of the line as a regular Special Release: Heritage Barrel. Whereas the other single barrels are handpicked barrels of whiskey that otherwise would have gone into Old No. 7 or the Jack Daniel's Bonded Rye, the Heritage Barrel releases are from a very different, quite separate stock. First, the barrels used double down on the Jack Daniel's barrel model, made with a low-temperature, long-duration toasting. Second, the entry proof for the whiskey into the barrel was cut to just 100.

For 2018 and 2019, the Heritage Barrel Special Releases were of Tennessee Whiskey, and this pair of whiskeys was a major step forward in persuading whiskey enthusiasts to stop shunning Jack Daniel's. I argue that Coy Hill (see opposite page) would not have been such a success among bloggers and writers had it not been for Heritage Barrel, because Heritage Barrel primed that community to pay closer attention to what was coming out of Lynchburg.

Later takes on the Heritage Barrel turned to Jack Daniel's rye. In 2023, the distillery took some of their regular rye whiskey, gave it a finish in the same kind of barrels used for the original Heritage Barrels, and out came the named-as-a-mouthful 100 proof Single Barrel Twice Barreled Heritage Barrel Rye. I suspect that Jack Daniel's is not settled with the Heritage Barrel, given that it has drawn on two mash bills already and may reach for the American Malt in the future, so speaking to its tasting notes is not useful. Suffice it to say that the Heritage Barrel releases have been reliably superb.

## Jack Daniel's Coy Hill Special Release Whiskeys

Perhaps no expression has done more to change the minds of whiskey enthusiasts about Jack Daniel's than 2021's Coy Hill Single Barrel and its successor, the 2022 Coy Hill Small Batch. I remember the revamping and expansion of the Single Barrel line causing some buzz among bloggers, writers, and fans, but the Coy Hill releases were met with outright applause.

Coy Hill is the highest prominence on the main Jack Daniel's Distillery property and hosts five rickhouses, all built in the 1960s. In covering the production process, I touched on how the floor that a given barrel is placed on can have a major impact on its maturation. The location of the rickhouse itself can have a similar influence, and exploring these climactic variations has become a theme in the 2020s for those whiskey companies with far-flung rickhouse properties. In Moore County, Coy Hill is just such a distinctive location relative to the other Jack Daniel's rickhouse complexes. In particular, barrels from the upper floors of those warehouses see severe water evaporation and soaring ABV numbers.

The Coy Hill Single Barrel of 2021 did not bear an age statement, but Chris Fletcher confirmed separately that the roughly 300 barrels chosen for the release were about nine years old. So, they were extra aged relative to normal single barrels and drawn from the fourth floor of the rickhouses to boot. This whiskey was bottled at cask strength, with those hundreds of individual barrels covering a range from 137.4 to 148.3 proof. The inaugural single barrel was a 750-ml bottle release, while the subsequent Coy Hill Small Batch of 2022 was in 375-ml bottles. As the story goes, in the creation of the Single Barrel, 55 barrels were found to have suffered such steep taxation from the angels that they had too little whiskey left to be considered for single barrel bottlings. The choice was made instead to batch these barrels together in a Small Batch release, and to do that in five separate batches with strengths of 143.6, 147.3, 149.8, 153.2, and 155.1 proof.

For Coy Hill, there is too much span within just the two releases that have come out to make tasting notes worthwhile. Suffice it to say, a Coy Hill whiskey is unmistakably Jack Daniel's, but is big bodied, bold, and intensely flavorful Jack Daniel's. These releases included the strongest ever to come out of Lynchburg, and they fit in nicely with the 2020s trend for high octane "Hazmat" whiskeys. Although Fletcher himself says that the Coy Hill release would have otherwise gone into Old No. 7, using the stock in this way really matched the pulse of American whiskey enthusiasts. As I prepared the final draft of this book, Jack Daniel's announced that a 2024 Coy Hill Single Barrel drawn from rickhouse 8 is set to be released, so these high proof Tennessee Whiskeys brought down from the distillery's highest perches will continue.

2024
SPECIAL
RELEASE
JACK DANIEL'S
UNIQUELY CRAFTED
HANDMADE BARRELS
SINGLE BARREL
Special Release
TENNESSEE
WHISKEY
COY HILL BARRELHOUSE 8
128.4 | 64.2
PROOF
% ALC/VOL
WHISKEY
DISTILLED & BOTTLED BY
JACK DANIEL DISTILLERY

2022
SPECIAL
RELEASE
JACK DANIEL'S
UNIQUELY CRAFTED
HANDMADE BARRELS
SMALL BATCH
Special Release
TENNESSEE
WHISKEY
10051638
COY HILL
HIGH PROOF
76.60 % ALC/VOL | 153.2 PROOF

JACK DANIEL'S
ORIGINAL RECIPE
Tennessee
APPLE
FINELY CRAFTED
APPLE LIQUEUR
FROM THE MAKERS OF JACK DANIEL'S
TENNESSEE WHISKEY
70cl e 35% Vol.
QUALITY & CRAFTSMANSHIP

## Jack Daniel's Tennessee Apple

As described by the label, this is an apple liqueur "blended with Jack Daniel's Tennessee Whiskey." The drink was released in 2019 to compete with similar offerings from Jim Beam and Crown Royal.

The source of the apple liqueur is undisclosed, but liqueurs in general are infusions. Some other distilled spirit is infused with apples and the kinds of spices one might find in apple pie, such as cinnamon, cloves, ginger, and/or nutmeg. Unlike apple brandy, which is distilled from hard cider and bottled at 40% ABV, apple liqueur is made *with* apples but not necessarily *from* apples and bottled at 35% ABV.

This apple liqueur is then blended with some Old No. 7. The end strength is 70 proof, the same as the original apple liqueur, so extra water is added either in blending or to one of the constituent ingredients. The result combines a little of the Jack Daniel's character with a strong current of Granny Smith apple, doing so without coming across as artificially flavored.

Whiskey enthusiasts are not fond of liqueurs of this type, and Tennessee Apple was no exception. Drinks writers and bloggers either excoriated it or, in the spirit of finding something kind to write, labeled it as fair in mixers or cocktails, but classed it as "ingredient-only." That is a fair description. Some flavored whiskeys and liqueurs are perfectly enjoyable on their own, especially on the rocks in summertime. Others have a strong appeal to casual drinkers, whether they like whiskey or not. Jack Apple falls into that class of bottles best used in concoctions, and not served up in and of itself.

## Jack Daniel's Tennessee Honey

Introduced in 2011, Tennessee Honey was not my first American whiskey-based honey liqueur. That was the granddaddy of the category, Wild Turkey Liqueur (now American Honey), which dates back to when I was just five years old! But I'm partial to sipping on these honey liqueurs, chilled and on the rocks, as a means of coping with the steamy summertime heat we must endure here in the sister states of Kentucky and Tennessee. Even though it marks me out as something of a heretic to my Kentucky neighbors, sometimes that bottle I pick up in June is Tennessee Honey. I like it that much.

When Tennessee Honey was released, Jack Daniel's had not unveiled a new whiskey since Single Barrel in 1997. That made it only their fifth expression in regular release for the American market, as well as the start of the current era that sees a steady flow of new bottlings coming out of Lynchburg.

Jack Daniel's Tennessee Honey is made in much the same way as Apple and Fire, by blending Old No. 7 Tennessee Whiskey with a liqueur, creating what is called a whiskey liqueur. What makes it different from the other two is that the liqueur is made with honey, and these whiskey-derived honey liqueurs, almost without exception, work out much better than other flavored whiskeys. Because it is so mellow, Old No. 7 works as a mate to honey liqueur especially well. Comparing it to Wild Turkey American Honey, the Wild Turkey liqueur has a contrasting element in the form of its bold, spicy character (that is "The Bird" for you). The Lynchburg way, on the other hand, complements the rich honeyed sweetness of the liqueur. The drink is honey-sweet in the main, but bright and clear on the palate, with modest Old No. 7 accents of banana and vanilla. The finish is especially well balanced, bringing along just as much sweetness as oak. Most important of all, flavored whiskeys have a way of tasting fake insofar as the flavor part is concerned, but good whiskey honey liqueurs do not, and this is a good whiskey honey liqueur.

Unlike Apple and Fire, which I would not bother with except as a cocktail ingredient, Tennessee Honey is worth having for sipping in its own right, and it is right up there with the original Wild Turkey product in my book. I'm told it is fantastic stirred into iced tea or lemonade, but I never bother with that. The expression is by far the most popular of the three Jack Daniel's flavored whiskey products, with experts and enthusiasts alike. It shipped over two million nine-liter cases in 2022, but as important as the numbers for me is that this is the one of the flavored trio that people actually talk about and reviewers give high marks to.

## Jack Daniel's Tennessee Fire

Between 2011 and 2013, sales of Fireball Cinnamon Whisky exploded a staggering thirtyfold. A craze like that prompts everyone who can get in on the act to chip away their own part of that market, which is exactly what whiskey makers great and small did. Jack Daniel's Tennessee Fire hit store and bar shelves in 2014, ready to slake the thirst of a phalanx of weekend binge drinkers.

Tennessee Fire is a cinnamon liqueur blended with Old No. 7, just like Honey and Apple. This is distinct from using Old No. 7 as the basis of the liqueur, because it means whiskey isn't the spirit infused with cinnamon. By comparison, Fireball is Canadian whisky infused with cinnamon and with other undisclosed sweeteners added.

My opinion on which process is superior is to make it a matter of someone else's opinion, because I don't have one. Tennessee Fire shares the qualities

JACK DANIEL'S
ORIGINAL RECIPE
Tennessee
HONEY
FINELY CRAFTED
HONEY LIQUEUR
FROM THE MAKERS OF JACK DANIEL'S
TENNESSEE WHISKEY
70cl 35% Vol. e
QUALITY & CRAFTSMANSHIP
ENJOY CHILLED

JACK DANIEL'S
ORIGINAL RECIPE
Tennessee
FIRE
FINELY CRAFTED
CINNAMON LIQUEUR
BLENDED WITH JACK DANIEL'S
TENNESSEE WHISKEY
1,0 Litre 35% Vol.

that made Fireball so popular: it tastes so much like a hot cinnamon candy that you don't really notice that it is booze. That was literal candy for a sizable chunk of the drinking public for a while, but that chunk had only a degree of overlap with Jack Daniel's die-hards and whiskey enthusiasts generally. Being a liqueur, it's bottled at 70 proof.

## Gone, but Not Forgotten

Because of the Bourbon Boom, it is rare to see a whiskey brand or expression of long standing discontinued. This current era usually sees the reverse, as many defunct old brands have been revived and pushed back into service. Existing expressions are often revamped instead of being abandoned, by gaining or losing an age statement for example. One such example was the Jack Daniel's Tennessee Straight Rye, which was essentially upgraded to Jack Daniel's Bonded Rye.

But Jack Daniel's is unique in that not only have they abandoned a handful of expressions in recent years, but these expressions are actually missed. In both my personal conversations and on internet forums, the nostalgia for some discontinued JD expressions is very real. While only die-hard nerds even noticed the departure of Jim Beam Green Label, folks who knew it continue to talk about Jack Daniel's Green Label. The lesson there is that if a whiskey bottle bore the name Jack Daniel's for decades, it is not easily forgotten by its public.

Another point of discontinuance is that a company can choose to stop making a given item, but it stays in the supply chain and then on store and bar shelves for months or even years after that. So, some recently discontinued expressions will continue to be available for either retail purchase or to try at the bar after this book sees print. When it comes to Jack Daniel's, *discontinued* takes a while to turn into *gone*.

### Lem Motlow's Sour Mash Whiskey

This dates to the earliest days of the company's revival, when Lem Motlow confronted a pressure familiar to any of today's craft distillers—getting a product on the market as soon as possible. Yet Motlow was militant about protecting the sterling reputation of his uncle's handiwork and the brand attached to it. He was not going to sell Jack Daniel's Old No. 7 before its time. The result was a young whiskey that Lem Motlow put his own name on. By the time it was withdrawn from the market in 1992, Lem Motlow's Sour Mash was positioned as the cheapest take on Old No. 7, but despite that was a niche product in limited distribution. Today, however, collectable bottles of the whiskey have (retail) price tags between $1,500 and $5,000 attached to them. I'm sure Lem would have been both proud and amused to see it.

## Jack Daniel's Green Label

When speaking of Green Label, historian Nelson Eddy regularly points out that Old No. 7 was not always labeled in black. Once upon a time, Jack Daniel's premiere product was labeled in green! The black label is a fixture of the modern era.

This version of JD Green Label was positioned between Lem Motlow Sour Mash and Old No. 7. It was blended and cut at 80 proof to be mellower and easier drinking than even its Black Label counterpart, which at the time was 90 proof. Whiskey expert Robin Robinson remembers it well: "[It was] aged in lower warehouses with less heat intensity, than [those] up on the hill. It was incredibly popular until they cut distribution in the US by half."

But as Jack Daniel's Black Label was cut down to 80 proof, the logic behind Green Label was clearly less compelling. Also, like Lem Motlow Sour Mash, the expression was very much a niche product by the time it reached its end in 2022, distributed to just a handful of states. In an era that sees the proliferation of premium and super-premium expressions, retaining this fan favorite (but still a somewhat down-market product) just did not make much sense.

## Jack Daniel's No 27 Gold

In both my talks with Jeff Arnett and in his published interviews, the whiskey he most often points to as a source of pride is No. 27 Gold. Like Gentleman Jack, it is a double mellowed whiskey, which was the origin point for calling it No. 27 (double + Old No. 7). The extra step was giving it a finish in specially constructed maple wood casks, which proved to be troublesome to fashion and prone to leakage. The difficulty in working with maple staves goes a long way to explaining why No. 27 did not get a longer life. Originally intended for the Asian market, it saw some wider international distribution, and I first got to try it at Whisky Live Paris in 2016. Although it has been discontinued, it is still available for retail at what are, for a collectable bottle, sometimes quite reasonable prices.

## Jack Daniel's Sinatra Select

Jack Daniel's has made much of its Frank Sinatra connection with limited edition whiskeys over the decades, but Sinatra Select was put into regular release and was the most accessible of the bunch. Like No. 27 Gold, which was created in the same era, Sinatra Select is based on a specialized cask. In this instance, those "Sinatra Barrels" were grooved on the inside. The grooves both increased the surface area inside the barrel and also exposed deeper layers of the wood that were less caramelized by toasting and charring. The result was that the Sinatra Barrels were as different from normal Jack Daniel's barrels as the Heritage Barrels continue to be.

Like the Tennessee Straight Rye, Sinatra Select is only recently discontinued and was very much still in the supply chain at the time of writing. Moreover, this up-market product was still available at rather normal prices.

## Jack Daniel's Tennessee Straight Rye

In 2012, Jack Daniel's introduced the public to their first new mash bill in a hundred years with an unaged rye whiskey. That release year was just after the trend of craft cocktails inspired by pre-Prohibition recipes took off like a rocket and swept most rye whiskey brands from store shelves. In the wake of the Rye Crunch of 2010 to 2011, many whiskey companies raised their rye game. There was also a fad for unaged "white" whiskeys and legal moonshines at the time, so the Jack Daniel's Unaged Rye fit right in.

Every two years after that, the company introduced successively older expressions, gradually exposing the public to rye whiskey done Lynchburg style. This culminated in their first mass market rye whiskey, Jack Daniel's Straight Rye, in 2017. Five years after distilling the first drop, the company was finally ready to introduce a rye positioned for the moderately priced part of the market, as this was the less expensive 90 proof counterpart to the Single Barrel Rye still in circulation. Underscoring its place on the product ladder, it came in the same bottle and label style as Jack Daniel's Old No. 7.

Most ryes look more like copper, a lighter coloring than the bourbon-style amber, and Jack Daniel's Rye is no exception. Taking in the aroma of the whiskey revealed a fresh, crisp scent, underlined by spearmint and fresh-cut grass. Orange zest gave the nose the main part of its fruity character, with the customary JD banana sitting as a faint background presence. The flavor, however, goes over to being very rye indeed, coming out on the palate with its cereals-forward. The liquid swings at you with a strong current of vanilla and peppery spices, a little orange zest, a thick banana slice, and a teaspoon of

JACK DANIEL'S
SINATRA SELECT
BOLD SMOOTH CLASSIC
TENNESSEE WHISKEY
SINATRA SELECT
CRAFTED FOR BOLD FLAVOR & EXCEPTIONAL SMOOTHNESS
JACK DANIEL'S
SINATRA SELECT
BOLD SMOOTH CLASSIC
TENNESSEE WHISKEY
DISTILLED & BOTTLED BY
JACK DANIEL DISTILLERY
LYNCHBURG TENNESSEE
45% ALC BY VOL/90 PROOF/1 LITER
SPECIAL EDITION

butterscotch. Following from that the conclusion is a strange one, as it runs a little nutty, but that finish is a light touch and fades fast.

After my first glass in 2017, I found myself thinking it was a shame Jack Daniel's didn't have this out back in 2011. If it had been around at that time, it would have garnered acclaim from bartenders desperate for a properly spicy rye with an authentic story to use in their cocktails. Given Frank Sinatra's connection with Old No. 7, Jack Daniel's Rye at that time would have become synonymous with a Rat Pack Manhattan. No one knew the Rye Craze was coming, though, so if wishes were fishes.

In October 2023, Brown-Forman announced that Jack Daniel's Straight Rye would be replaced by the newly released Bonded Rye. Yet at the time of writing, this product is still widely available. Inquiries with some folks in liquor distribution revealed they could still get it, so Jack Daniel's Straight Rye isn't gone ... yet. Fans interested in having a little piece of company history should give some thought to snagging a bottle and storing it away as an unopened collectable.

EVERY DROP MADE IN LYNCHBURG TENNESSEE
JACK DANIEL'S
BARREL AGED
RYE
MOORE Cº
Tennessee
STRAIGHT
RYE WHISKEY
DISTILLED & BOTTLED BY
JACK DANIEL DISTILLERY
LYNCHBURG, TENN. USA
70cl 45% Vol.
QUALITY AND CRAFTSMANSHIP SINCE 1866

EVERY DROP MADE IN

DANIEL'S
Old
No.7
BRAND

## Acknowledgments

The acknowledgments made for my last book somehow went awry between submission and typesetting, which makes expressing some gratitude especially important this time around. Keeping that in mind, I wish to start with the folks at Cider Mill Press for expressing confidence in me by giving me the project you are now reading. Not only is writing a book about a single distillery a substantial undertaking, even when that distillery is Jack Daniel's, but this is also intended as the pilot for a larger series. To quote the president, this is a big f-ing deal, so thank you.

Next are the folks representing the entity whose cooperation was essential: Brown-Forman. Underscoring just how difficult it is to narrow the focus like this, if Brown-Forman had chosen not to cooperate or the people concerned had merely been begrudging in that cooperation, there would have been no book. I ran into some of that minimal style of cooperation from less important organizations along the way, which only proved the point. I would like to thank the individuals who generously shared their time and stories during the research for this book. This work is entirely my own. While employees of Brown-Forman Corporation and Jack Daniel's kindly made themselves available for interviews, neither they nor their organizations had any editorial control or influence over the content. Their participation does not imply endorsement or sponsorship of this book. In particular, I want to thank Chris Fletcher and Nelson Eddy, who were both very busy with whiskey-related travel during the summer of 2024, for sparing me some time. Minh Le and Serena Helm at Finn Partners were most patient with my steady requests for imagery, and finally Svend Jansen had the patience of a saint given my appetite for facts and figures.

For more than a decade, I have had an interest in talking to creative folks such as actors, artists, and musicians about whiskey culture, and this book gave me the opportunity to put that interest to work. That said, I had to reach out to all new people for the most part. Maarten Statius Muller helped me find some of the artists in question, and I want to thank the producers of Roast Battle Chicago for pointing a devoted fan in the right direction for comics.

Some of my colleagues were kind enough to share their thoughts with me, which is always a refreshing reminder that this business can still be cooperative rather than competitive. Diving into these things with Robin Robinson is often its own reward, and it was a pleasure to bring Tom Wilmes, Christine Gallagher, Adrian Miller, and Ed Escott into the work.

Jeff Arnett has moved onto his own enterprise now, but he was generous with his time and happy to look backward with me for an afternoon in Townsend, Tennessee. If you've never been there, I strongly recommend it, if for no other reason than it is the Smokies sans Gatlinburg. I also contacted Dr. Pat Heist, esteemed fermentation consultant and cofounder of Wilderness Trail Distillery, to delve into some of the finer points of fermentation and provide an outside viewpoint. As it happened, those points were more useful as background than as quotes, making it particularly necessary to thank him here. I should also nod to the folks at the *St. Louis Post-Dispatch* and the Tennessee State Library & Archives for being so cooperative with me when my inquiries were clearly not everyday requests.

Finally, I must thank my son, Luke. This was the first summer that he was finally old enough that when I asked him to give me a couple of uninterrupted hours to write, he was happy to entertain himself and give me that time. That made a substantial difference in the quality of the work, as well as opened the way to a stress-free 30-day final stretch before deadline. Besides, he is the main reason I work so hard.

BEHIND THE BOTTLE
JACK DANIEL'S
RICHARD THOMAS

## About the Author

Richard Thomas is a native and resident of Kentucky, which is the basis of his whiskey writing. As a teenager, he discovered the ruins of what would later become Woodford Reserve, Castle & Key, and Glenn's Creek Distillery. Some urban exploring in these spots was the starting point for a lifetime spent enjoying and studying whiskey, with some of those tales appearing in his book *Whiskey Stories*.

Although Thomas grew up around horses and bourbon, he spent several years living in Portugal, where he broke into writing about whiskey as the Kentucky bourbon guy who could also say something about Scotch and Irish whiskey. Living in the midst of the fortified wines of Portugal and Spain (he has written a short book about Port wine) deepened his palate, as well his understanding of sensory science and how liquor is made, and he briefly ran a cask-sourcing consultancy abroad.

It was also while living in Europe that Thomas founded The Whiskey Reviewer website, in 2011, and continues as owner-editor. Under his stewardship, the website's team has produced work that has been cited, quoted, and reprinted by the American Distilling Institute, *The Atlantic*, BroBible, Cheat Sheet, Drinkhacker, Eater, Foodista, *Islay Daily News*, MarketWatch, Mode, *The New York Times*, *NY Daily News*, Toronto.com, *The Washington Post*, WRAL.com, and many others. As a freelancer, Thomas wrote about spirits for *Chilled*, Inside Hook, *Paste*, and VinePair.

Thomas is also the author of *American Whiskey*, *The Whiskey Cookbook*, and *Whiskey Stories*. When he is not writing, you might find him building a house, banging a heavy bag, or hauling a ruck in Daniel Boone National Forest.

## About Cider Mill Press Book Publishers

Cider Mill Press publishes exceptional books that combine creativity and craftsmanship. As an imprint of HarperCollins Focus, we specialize in premium cookbooks, cocktail and spirits guides, and illustrated gift books, all distinguished by compelling content, striking design, and a commitment to quality in every detail. Cider Mill Press sets the standard for books that inform, inspire, and elevate everyday moments. Learn more at cidermillpress.com.

"Where Good Books Are Ready for Press"
501 Nelson Place
Nashville, Tennessee 37214 USA